LANGUAGE
of THE

heart.

IMPROVING
EVERY
RELATIONSHIP

JOHN R. STEWARD

*To my wife, Torild Steward,
who has been my partner in
the Language of the Heart.
Your support and love have
been vital to my life.*

TABLE OF CONTENTS

FORWARD

I have been aware for a number of years now that one of Pastor Steward's passions is helping people learn to communicate in ways that promote resonant relational and familial health and productivity. Having counseled countless church members over the course of his pastoral history, and perhaps experienced most intensely when working with couples; Pastor Steward has come to realize that communication determines the intrinsic core qualities of any relationship.

Can we speak from our own feeling base? Can we use "I" statements? Can we reflect back what the other is attempting to share without jumping in with defensive retorts? Are we allowed to feel our feelings rather than be guided to the "right" or "acceptable" feelings based on the family milieu? Can we offer attentive listening that promotes authentic, vulnerable sharing that produces a warm, intimate connection that reflects God's love? Can we respect the sovereignty of the other? Feel known and understood? Elicit mutual respect? Create a spirit of cooperation? Promote interactions that contain and soothe our souls? Can we offer full attention, eye contact, and warm receptive facial expressions? Can we become aware of and avoid the destructive quality of name-calling, shaming/blaming, and accusing statements? Can we avoid offering unsolicited advice? Can we curtail asking too many questions? Being an amateur therapist? Being a caretaker? Comparing our children? Speaking in a sarcastic tone? Giving lectures? Offering negative prophecy?

As a psychotherapist working with these concepts in my private practice, I am deeply encouraged and impressed with Pastor Steward's committed and enduring drive to facilitate the acquisition and effective use of communication skills.

Integrating the application of communication skills with biblical truths, Pastor Steward has compiled a manuscript of his presentations and sermons entitled most aptly and coined by him, "Language of the Heart." The guidebook you hold in your hands is the distillation of his various communication concepts. It is Pastor Steward's hope that this book, and eventually a website dedicated to the "Language of the Heart," will improve relationships and promote communication competency by reaching an audience well beyond the bounds of our own church.

I applaud Pastor Steward's diligent efforts and foresee this book and its contents being a blessing and a useful tool to all who embrace its precepts.

DR. PIPER GLASIER, MSW, LCSW, PSY.D

INTRODUCTION

For many years as a pastor, I have stood with people in some of the worst times of their lives. Some moments have been thrust upon these people by health issues or other aspects that were outside of their control. At other times, I have watched people create their own problems in the relationships they have with others. Whether those relationships are at home, work, or in the community, many people fail in their pursuits and never seem to be able to succeed as they might desire.

In fact, I have watched some of the smartest people with very advanced educations unable to succeed in the relationships in their lives. Many of these well-educated people often fail to accomplish things you would think they should accomplish. While some people are incredibly intelligent, they lack in a basic level of "emotional intelligence." I have seen people who have climbed the corporate ladder or who have amassed a fortune unable to have successful relationships or accomplish their goals. In other words, there are many well-educated, powerful, or wealthy failures in life.

They cannot accomplish their goals because people do not want to work with them. They have multiple marriages because no one can live with them. Their adult children are estranged from them and rarely speak to them. What went wrong?

Often the problem roots back to what I call the "Language of the Heart." The Language of the Heart contains biblical principles which develop your character and your ability to communicate effectively with others and thereby improve every relationship. The problems many people have are found in character flaws, or addiction, or just in the lack of being able to listen to others. However, when the principles of the Language of the Heart are lived out, amazing things begin to happen. People want to be married to you and stay married to you. People want to hire you and promote you. People want to be your friend and remain in a friendship relationship with you.

So this is what my book is about. Using the Language of the Heart can help to develop our character and our ability to communicate, to solve problems in healthy ways, and to improve every relationship so we can succeed in our various endeavors. It can help to develop character traits which are healthy and contribute positively to the lives of those around us. This has been a large part of my ministry; working with people and helping them live out the Language of the Heart. My prayer is that this book will help to strengthen your abilities and help you overall as well.

PASTOR JOHN R. STEWARD

CHAPTER ONE
WHAT IS THE LANGUAGE OF THE HEART?

What is the Language of the Heart? In many ways, the Language of the Heart is a language which, when used and understood, can make a great impact on the relationships in our lives. Too often, the Language of the Heart is like a foreign language. Have you ever been in a situation where someone was speaking to you in a language you didn't understand?

Years ago, I was in Norway traveling to various cities such as Trondheim and Bergen. I was with family members who spoke Norwegian. We stopped at a restaurant to have lunch, and when we were done everyone went back to the car. I said I would first go to the bathroom before getting in the car. They left the restaurant and I found myself trying to find the bathroom in a foreign country, not knowing the word for bathroom in Norwegian. Well, I had an interesting time trying to make myself understood.

This is the situation with the Language of the Heart. It is often a language not everyone understands. The Language of the Heart is a foreign language and we need to study and learn it. Through this book, I hope to help you learn to translate this language. We might look at this as the Rosetta Stone Training for the heart and for relationships. The wonderful thing about the Language of the Heart is its principles come right out of God's Word – the Bible. It is wonderful to know God has created principles which, when learned and followed with great discipline, can improve every relationship in our lives.

So together, let's learn a new language from the principles of God's Word!

LIVING THE LANGUAGE OF THE HEART

The Language of the Heart is the ability to have feelings and to share these feelings. It is the ability to recognize feelings in others and be able to listen to them. It is the ability to listen and not be self-defensive, to have values such as honesty and respect for others, and to have boundaries with others and with yourself.

You can be highly intelligent with many post-graduate degrees, but if you cannot speak the Language of the Heart, it will be difficult to have successful relationships with family, friends and co-workers. Many parents spend a great deal of time concerning themselves with their children's education, their homework, their test scores, their grades and their SAT scores. But if your child does not learn the Language of the Heart, your child's life will be more difficult than it needs to be.

Why is it so difficult for people to speak and communicate in the Language of the Heart? One reason is our broken condition. Because we are broken people, we are filled with pride, arrogance and selfishness. We are filled with a desire to be served and not to serve; a desire to receive and not give. We believe we are entitled and we don't possess the ability to die to ourselves. In a word, it is our sin that prevents us from speaking this language.

THE FOUNDATION OF THE LANGUAGE OF THE HEART IS LOVE

The Language of the Heart begins with love. Being able to love God and to love others is the foundation of the Language of the Heart. The religious leaders came to Jesus with a very specific question. They asked Him which was the greatest of all the commandments that had been given to Moses. Jesus answered this question with a revolutionary idea:

"Teacher, which commandment in the law is the greatest?" He said to him," 'You shall love the Lord your God with all your heart, and with all your soul, and with all your mind.' This is the greatest and first commandment. And a second is like it: 'You shall love your neighbor as yourself.' On these two commandments hang all the laws and the prophets."
– Matthew 22:36-40

This is the key to the Language of the Heart, and it reaches beyond the intellectual level. It begins by loving the Lord your God with your heart, soul and mind. In order to do this, we first have to know God really does love us. So many people walk around with a deficit in this area of being loved. Perhaps in their childhood they were abused verbally, physically or sexually. Maybe it was an alcoholic parent. Maybe it was a family where you were taught not to have feelings but to buck up and be tough, or just that life itself has wounded you; or you were in a family where you were made to feel stupid. On and on the list goes. Often it is a trauma that is never really healed. When this happens, many people simply bury their pain and go on with life the best they can. This results in a deficit of love, which makes it difficult to love God and to love others. It means the Language of the Heart is a foreign language, not a native tongue.

The Language of the Heart begins with experiencing God's love – not just knowing about it, but experiencing this love in a genuine way. This is what often happens on a Cursillo weekend. Cursillo is an international ministry of Christian renewal. The name "Cursillo" means "short course" in Spanish because it is a short course in the Christian faith, which usually takes place over a weekend. Cursillo started in Spain in the 1930's and has spread all over the world, arriving in Southern California in about 1989. Our congregation at Mount of Olives in Mission Viejo, California, has sent over four hundred people to these weekends. The result is that people have a genuinely powerful encounter with the love of God in a very rich and meaningful way.

To begin learning the Language of the Heart means experiencing the love of God, and then you will be able to love those around you using this new language. We are not talking about religion, but rather a relationship with God in which we experience His love. It means allowing this love of God to seep into the places of hurt in your life and allowing Him to heal you. When the pain that caused you to bury your own pain is healed, you begin to experience the love of God, and this is when you can learn this new language. Perhaps it is time for you to take steps which will bring about this healing, such as seeing a professional Christian counselor to help make this happen in your life, or to go to a 12-step program and deal with the issues of addiction that have blocked you from feeling this love of God. You may have been searching for it through addiction but it hasn't worked, so now it's time to be healed and experience this love of God. This is where the Language of the Heart begins – experiencing the love of God. That leads us to the next step – loving others. The Language of the Heart is to love others in the same way God loves us.

THE LANGUAGE OF THE HEART IS TO LOVE OTHERS LIKE GOD LOVES US

In I John 3:14, we read these words:

"We know that we have passed from death to life because we love one another. Whoever does not love abides in death."

Once we experience the love of God through Jesus Christ, there is fruit. The fruit of God's love shows and it is given away to others. At this point, we are in position to learn the skills of this new Language of the Heart. However, when we do not practice love, it brings death to every relationship and we will be dead on the inside. Our relationships will be dead. There will be a lack of life in our lives. When we experience this love of God through Jesus, it changes us. We cannot be the same demanding person. We cannot be the same defensive person. We cannot be the same insensitive person. In other words, our hearts need to change.

THE LANGUAGE OF LOVE REQUIRES A NEW HEART

In Ezekiel 11:19-20, we read:

"I will give them one heart, and put a new spirit within them; I will remove the heart of stone from their flesh and give them a heart of flesh, so that they may follow my statutes and keep my ordinances and obey them. Then they shall be my people, and I will be their God."

Sometimes the problem we have in the learning of the Language of the Heart is our heart is cold and hard. Sometimes our families have taught us this. They said to us, "Stop crying or I will give you something to really cry about." In such moments, we were taught to bury our feelings and this makes it very difficult to learn the Language of the Heart because this language is feeling-based.

Sometimes we have trouble learning this new language because of the way the world works. I heard about a family where the father complained about how difficult things were at work, and his daughter said, "Daddy, why don't you just tell your boss you want to be in the slow group?" The father had to explain the real world doesn't work like that. In the real world, you are taught to be tough and strong, and you are expected to bury your feelings. They would never teach the Language of the Heart in the military. The thinking is you can't have soldiers on the battlefield dealing with their feelings, which is understandable. Yet in recent years, we've seen some of the highest rates of suicide in the military. Obviously, the culture doesn't allow for people to have feelings; they must bury them and go it alone – with extremely damaging results. In so many areas of life, the Language of the Heart is submerged.

We need a new heart – a heart of flesh and not stone; a heart where we can feel and respect our own feelings and the feelings of others. When we can do this, we are beginning to learn the Language of the Heart. When our hearts have been damaged in our lives, we have an emotional heart problem. Our physical hearts might be just fine, but it is possible to have an emotional heart problem where we have a hard heart. How do you know if you have a hardening of the heart?

You believe:

- Weakness is bad.
- Emotions should be kept to yourself.
- There are certain feelings and emotions that are bad and unhealthy.
- Crying is a sign someone is not doing well and they must be rescued from their tears by changing the subject or telling a funny story.
- Instead of hearing someone's pain, we try to help them solve their problem.
- We know our heart is hard when we say to someone, "You shouldn't feel that way."
- We know we lack Language of the Heart when we say, "I know how you feel."
- When we demand "our way or the highway," there is a lack of genuine kindness within us.

God wants to replace our heart of stone with a heart of flesh. In other words, the Language of the Heart is to love like God loves us.

The Language of the Heart says all feelings are good. It is important to keep in mind feelings are not the same as opinions. Many people use the terms "feelings" and "opinions" interchangeably, saying, for example, "I *feel* we should try a different restaurant for a change." Feelings are emotions I feel, while opinions are my thoughts and ideas. Feelings can be described as the emotions of being sad or happy, angry or hurt. There is no such thing as a bad feeling or emotion, and you cannot "know" what someone else is feeling because you are not that person.

In the Language of the Heart, you only want to hear the emotions of others, knowing that listening is all that is needed. In the Language of the Heart, you know you don't have to take ownership for the emotions of others. In the Language of the Heart, you know burying your emotions and feelings is basically unhealthy and dysfunctional. Jesus was able to do all of this, and we will see how He did it in the chapters to come.

FROM A HEART OF STONE TO A HEART OF FLESH

When we live in this way, we are moving from having a heart of stone to a heart of flesh. Relationships begin to heal and be restored. People want to befriend us, or to be married to us and stay married to us. This is the benefit of the Language of the Heart.

The love of God is foundational to the Language of the Heart. When we experience God's love, it changes us. Our values change, our priorities change, our attitudes change. We have set aside our pride and arrogance and have replaced them with humility. We are no longer interested in being right but are more concerned someone is treated right. Our drive to succeed is replaced by our desire to serve others. This is what emerges from an experience with the love of God.

As Proverbs 12:15-23 points out:

"Fools think their own way is right, but the wise listen to advice. Fools show their anger at once, but the prudent ignore an insult. Whoever speaks the truth gives honest evidence, but a false witness speaks deceitfully. Rash words are like sword thrusts, but the tongue of the wise brings healing. Truthful lips endure forever, but a lying tongue lasts only a moment. Deceit is in the mind of those who plan evil, but those who counsel peace have joy. No harm happens to the righteous, but the wicked are filled with trouble. Lying lips are an abomination to the LORD, but those who act faithfully are His delight. One who is clever conceals knowledge, but the mind of a fool broadcasts folly."

Let's break this down further:

- *Fools think their own way is right, but the wise listen to advice.* Those who lack a working ability with the Language of the Heart think their way is right. It is their way or the highway. But those who speak the Language of the Heart can listen to advice. They are open and teachable.
- *The prudent ignore an insult.* What would happen in our relationships if we did not become defensive? What

would happen if we ignored insults? You can do this when you experience the love of God, because now there is a confidence within us. We are no longer dependent on what others think because we have the love of God living in our hearts. Only the person who has this confidence can really do this, and the result is they are often able to navigate through difficult conversations.

- *Truthful lips endure forever, but a lying tongue lasts only a moment… Lying lips are an abomination to the LORD, but those who act faithfully are His delight.* When we tell lies, we are trying to get out of a bad situation; our pride and ego are at work. It never helps us. Those who speak the Language of the Heart are honest even when it is painful and they are being held accountable. They tell the truth and in so doing they build trust and have long-lasting relationships.

- *Deceit is in the mind of those who plan evil, but those who counsel peace have joy. No harm happens to the righteous, but the wicked are filled with trouble.* There are those who are often looking for a fight, wanting to prevail. They end up manipulating others and the result is constant drama in their lives. There are those who have to have things done their way and there is no other way. One of the reasons we have arguments is many times we are trying to convince others we are right, they are wrong, and they are trying to do the same to us. Those who speak the Language of the Heart are more interested in trying to understand than being understood. The one who speaks the Language of the Heart works toward reconciliation resulting in peace and joy.

- *One who is clever conceals knowledge, but the mind of a fool broadcasts folly.* To conceal knowledge simply means that someone is able to control himself. There are those who are proud to say "I speak my mind" which results in saying things that damages other people and strains their relationships with them. The person who speaks the Language of the Heart understands they need to wait for the right moment and to say what they think in ways that build up and not tear down.

Having a heart of flesh is essential to building our relationships. Pastor Joel Pankow of Trinity Evangelical Church in Bayside, Michigan,[1] tells this story to make the point:

In a backyard there once lived an apple tree and a thorn bush. The apple tree produced nice, juicy apples that everyone liked to eat. Kids would climb up the tree and pluck the apples. Worms would eat the ones that fell on the ground. Birds would peck away at the fruit from the top. The owner would also prune and spray the tree to make sure it produced lots of fruit for the neighborhood. In the corner, about 50 yards from the apple tree stood a thorn bush. Nobody messed with the thorn bush. One day, old Jimmy Johnson ran his bike into it, but after he got all cut up, he never made the same mistake again. Nobody picked any fruit off of it; everyone left it alone. At first the apple tree liked all the attention. But after about ten years, it started becoming envious of the thorn bush. It said to the thorn bush, "You know, I'm sick of everyone always climbing on me and picking my fruit. The master is always trimming me, putting smelly manure around my trunk, and making a fuss over me. I wish they'd go somewhere else. Better yet, I wish I was a thorn bush, and then everyone would leave me alone." The thorn bush then looked at the apple tree and said, "Don't be a fool! Bite your bark! Look at me! I don't do anyone a bit of good. I feed nobody. I look ugly. All I do is harm. The Master didn't plant me here; I'm just a wild weed. The only good I do is filling up some space in the yard. I would trade all the thorns in the world to have one child climb my branches, to have the Master trim my branches, and to produce some fruit."

Which one will we be; the Apple Tree or the Thorn Bush? We want to be the Apple Tree, but too many times we are the Thorn Bush that repels people from us, and prevents us from having meaningful and healthy relationships. In order to be the Apple Tree we need a new heart. Ask Jesus to give you a new heart; a heart of flesh. Open yourself up to being able to be taught the concepts of the Language of the Heart so you can learn from God's Word, the principles which improve your relationships.

CHAPTER TWO
BEING ABLE TO FEEL FEELINGS

In many ways, the Language of the Heart is like a foreign language. It does not come to us naturally but is something that needs to be learned. In the previous chapter, we learned the Language of the Heart is the ability to have and share emotions and feelings, even though the world tells us to bury our feelings.

THE WORLD SEES FEELINGS AND EMOTIONS AS WEAKNESSES

The world does not practice the Language of the Heart. In fact, the opposite is true. Many of our families, our workplaces and even our friendships are designed around the idea that we should ignore and bury our feelings; we should be like robots and machines. Many families do not allow expressions of feelings.

For example, on August 20, 1989, Lyle and Erik Menendez shot their parents to death in their Beverly Hills family home. Lyle was 21 and Erik was 18 years of age. They had grown up in New Jersey but relocated with their parents, Jose and Kitty Menendez, when they were in high school. Their father was a hard-driving, successful and extremely wealthy man. He was highly demanding of his sons. They later alleged they were significantly abused all their lives, even sexually abused by their father, and their mother was a manipulative and unstable drug addict. There is no excuse for what they did, and it is an extreme example of what happens in such families. However, it did happen in their family.

On the stand, Lyle Menendez explained their father's philosophy that he would often recite to his sons. It is a philosophy many in our culture agree with and follow, one that many parents teach their children. From memory, Lyle recited, "Today, I will be master of my emotions. If I feel depressed, I will sing. If I feel sad, I will laugh. If I feel ill, I will double my labor. If I feel fear, I will plunge ahead. If I feel inferior, I will wear new garments. If I feel poverty, I will think of wealth to come. If I feel insignificant, I will remember my goals. I will be master of my emotions." Later, while still on the stand, Lyle testified that his father believed "a great sign of weakness is to display emotion."

Many people believe in order for you to be successful in life, you need to bury your feelings and become like a machine. I have seen many people live according to this philosophy and I can tell you it is a formula for failure. This worldly thinking will damage your relationships with your spouse, your children, your friends and co-workers. This is not a healthy way to live your life; nor is it what God intended for you either.

JESUS TEACHES BY EXAMPLE ABOUT HOW TO FEEL OUR EMOTIONS

Let's look at the principles of the Language of the Heart

found in God's Word. As we begin, we can look to our Lord and Savior, Jesus Christ. God became human in Jesus. Jesus is fully God and fully man. Let's look at how He lived out the Language of the Heart.

One day, one of Jesus' friends, Lazarus, became ill and was dying. They called on Jesus so that He might heal him, but He was delayed in coming to be with Lazarus. By the time Jesus arrived, Lazarus had died. Lazarus' sister, Mary, was actually upset with Jesus and said so, which is another example of the Language of the Heart in the story. Watch now how Jesus responded. He didn't become upset with Mary and defend Himself, which He could easily have done. Instead, He allowed Mary the freedom to express herself, which is what the Language of the Heart is all about.

> *"When Mary came where Jesus was and saw Him, she knelt at His feet and said to Him, "Lord, if You had been here, my brother would not have died." When Jesus saw her weeping, and the Jews who came with her also weeping, He was greatly disturbed in spirit and deeply moved. He said, "Where have you laid him?" They said to Him, "Lord, come and see." Jesus began to weep." – John 11:32-35*

Jesus wept! Jesus' tears are an example to us that it's okay to cry, we are meant to have emotions and to express our emotions and feelings. Mary is critical of Jesus and He doesn't defend Himself. Instead, He is sensitive to the pain of those around Him, and to His own pain, and He cries. This is the Language of the Heart.

In Hebrews 5:7 we read:

"In the days of His flesh, Jesus offered up prayers and supplications, with loud cries and tears, to the One who was able to save Him from death, and He was heard because of His reverent submission."

This teaches us *Jesus* was fluent in the Language of the Heart. He did not bury His feelings and pretend they did not exist, but instead expressed *"loud cries and tears."* He gives us this particular permission to have feelings and emotions and to express them as well. If Jesus could cry, then why do we deny giving ourselves permission to cry?

This is crucial to learning to speak the Language of the Heart, because if you cannot express your feelings or allow others to express their emotions, you will not be able to speak this foreign language. This is one of the foundations of the Language of the Heart; emotions are good and they need to be expressed. So, once we change our philosophical view of life from saying emotions are bad, to understanding emotions are healthy and good and should be expressed; then how do we speak this foreign language?

USING THE LANGUAGE OF THE HEART

In Ephesians 4:26, we read:

"Be angry but do not sin; do not let the sun go down on your anger."

The first thing we see here is it is all right to be angry. Anger is a normal emotion; which can and should be expressed. God is the author of our emotions. He created emotions. They are meant to give us release from the pains of life and help us to celebrate its joys. In this passage in Ephesians, we learn even anger is a healthy emotion. It is what we do with our anger that matters. If it causes us to harm someone, this is a misuse of anger, but to say out loud we are angry is healthy. That's what Mary was doing when Lazarus died. She was telling Jesus about her anger. He didn't tell her she shouldn't say this; nor did He try to rescue her from her emotions or defend Himself. He simply allowed her to have her emotions.

This passage from Ephesians is saying we are allowed to have our feelings, and we are to do something with our feelings of anger. We are meant to work at reconciliation. We are not meant to take our anger and meditate on it or to dwell on it. We are not meant to use it to confirm we are victims and everyone is out to harm us. No, the Language of the Heart means we are to work at reconciliation. This means to work at settling problems with others in such a way that a relationship is restored, and it should be done the right way. We aren't supposed to wait for weeks and months, but rather to do it as soon as possible. We need to bring reconciliation that very same day before the sun goes down, if possible. It says we sin when we let the sun go down on our anger. Notice the sin is not the emotion, but rather the failure to work at restoring the relationship. This is because when we refuse to work at relationships, our refusal keeps broken relationships broken.

In *Guiding Your Family in a Misguided* World, Dr. Anthony T. Evans[2] tells the story of Two Monks:

It seems that two monks were walking down a long country road. They were going to another village to help the farmers bring in the crops. Along the way they saw an old woman sitting next to a river. She was upset because without a bridge she could not cross the river. The first monk offered to help her. He said he would be willing to carry her across the river if she would like. She agreed and the two monks joined their arms and carried her across the river. After they set her down, she went on her way.

The monks resumed their travels, and the second monk began to complain. He said, "Look at my clothes they are filthy from carrying that woman across the river. And my back still hurts from lifting her. I can feel it getting stiff with every mile we walk." The first monk acknowledged what he heard by smiling and then nodded his head. After traveling a few more miles up the road, the second monk complained some more. "My back is worse and it is all because we carried that old woman across the river! I cannot go any farther, I am in too much pain." The first monk looked at the other monk who was lying on the ground complaining. "Have you wondered why you don't hear me complaining?" he asked. "Your back hurts because you never set the woman down, you are still carrying her, but I set her down five miles ago" the first monk said.

This is what many of us are like in dealing with our families. We are like the second monk who cannot let go. We hold the pain of the past over our loved ones' heads like a club, or when we want to get the upper hand, we remind them every once in a while of the burden we still carry because of something they did years ago. The Language of the Heart means we let go of our anger first by expressing it, and then we learn to forgive, which is how we build bridges of reconciliation. The Language of the Heart is the ability to listen to the emotions of another and build bridges of reconciliation there as well.

THE GREAT NEED FOR ACTIVE LISTENING

James 1:19 informs us:

"You must understand this, my beloved: let everyone be quick to listen, slow to speak, slow to anger…"

What a wonderful formula this is! This is the Language of the Heart lived out in a practical way. It means we listen more than we talk, and we try to understand more than we try to be understood.

When we argue with someone, most of the time we're trying to make our point. We believe we are right, and if I can just help you see that I'm right, we won't have a problem. But the other person is thinking the exact same thing. What would happen if instead of trying to make our point, we spent our time trying to understand deeply what the other person is saying? We don't have to agree with them, but if we just really try to hear them, it would actually end an argument. This means hearing them to the point where we could give a report on what they said, and we would find there would be very few arguments. There's a name for this. It is called active listening.

There is a difference between passive listening and active listening. When I teach people in counseling or before an audience, people sit and listen. Sometimes they nod their heads in agreement. They are looking at me and they seem to be paying attention; hearing what I'm saying. This is called passive listening. You can see passive listening in one-on-one conversations. Someone is talking and the other person is responding by nodding or smiling as if they understand. But here is the problem with passive listening: you don't really know if the other person has actually heard you. They might be thinking, "I can't wait to get to breakfast after the worship service." They might be thinking about what they will serve next week at their Super Bowl party, or they might be thinking about Maui. There is no way we can know we're really being heard when they listen passively.

Active listening is different because it actually sends a message back that you are heard. For example, if someone were to say, "I really had a tough day at work today – there is so much to get done and we don't have enough people to do it," the active listener would respond by saying, "So you had a really tough day at work...too much to do and not enough help to get it done." And the other person would respond by saying, "Yeah...that's it." They would have felt heard and understood, and this is what the Language of the Heart is about. What too many people do in that moment is to look for a solution. They would say, "Well, why don't you tell your boss that he needs to hire more people?" This is not active listening, nor is it the Language of the Heart. Active listening is what can heal relationships, prevent arguments, and build deeper relationships. This is why James says, "Let everyone be quick to listen, slow to speak, slow to anger."

When you can do this kind of active listening, you can move on to find solutions to disagreements. Allowing others to share their thoughts and emotions without us trying to defend ourselves or change them; just truly hearing them will cause them to want to work at reconciliation. Remember one of the aspects of the Language of the Heart is the ability to listen to the emotions of others and build bridges of reconciliation with them.

AFTER ACTIVE LISTENING WE CAN MOVE ON TO RECONCILIATION

We learn in Matthew 5:23-24:

"So when you are offering your gift at the altar, if you remember that your brother or sister has something against you, leave your gift there before the altar and go; first be reconciled to your brother or sister, and then come and offer your gift."

The Language of the Heart means we work at trying to reconcile relationships. This is what Jesus is teaching us here in the Sermon on the Mount. He says if you are on your way to church to offer your offering to the Lord, and on the way you remember your neighbor or family member is upset with you; you are to stop, go back home, and be reconciled to that person before you give God anything. You cannot truly give to God when there is a broken relationship in your life. God wants you to get this right first because then you will be able to truly focus on your worship to God.

Notice in this passage from Matthew 5, it did not say "if you have something against your brother or sister," but rather if someone has "something against you." At first sight, this doesn't seem fair. We could understand this if we had something against someone, but to say we must bring reconciliation when someone is upset and angry with us seems to be too much to ask. This doesn't seem to make sense. What it points out to us is how much God wants us to bring healing to the relationships in our lives. He wants us to have loving, healed and wholesome relationships before an offering is brought to Him and He wants this done the right way – don't let the sun go down on your anger. However, it should be noted if you are in an abusive relationship, you need professional help. You should create boundaries and sometimes those boundaries include loving others from afar. We are never meant by God to excuse or tolerate abuse. You are created in the image of God and were never meant to be abused and have your dignity destroyed.

This is the Language of the Heart. When we work at reconciliation, we are speaking the Language of the Heart. The world would tell us to be passive-aggressive. The world would tell us to be vindictive, but Jesus teaches us the Language of the Heart and says we should work at reconciliation.

The Language of the Heart is the ability to listen to the emotions of others and to build bridges of reconciliation.

CHAPTER THREE
RESOLVING CONFLICT

In the previous chapter, we talked about active listening as a key to improving every relationship in the Language of the Heart. By actively listening, we learned it sends a message back to the other person we heard them. However, it has to be more than simply looking at the other person and nodding our heads. We have to send what I call a "10-4 message."

During graduate school and my internship in Pennsylvania, I drove across the United States to and from California a few times. In those days, CB radios were very popular and I had one in my car. During long days driving across the country, I would talk with truckers on the CB radio and it was a lot of fun. In fact, my handle (a call name you'd use on the CB radio instead of your real name) was "Preacher Man." When you use a CB radio or HAM radio, you have to speak in a certain way so the person on the other end knows you heard them, and your communication has ended. One such phrase was "10-4." This meant you heard the message the other person was sending. One reason this becomes important is because the other person can't see you and doesn't know if you're still on the air or if you've understood what they've said. When you say "10-4," you are telling them you understood what they had just communicated. The same is true with our communication in our relationships. We need to send them a "10-4" message so they will know they're being heard and understood. Active listening is meant to be a "10-4" message because it communicates the other person was heard and understood.

Being able to engage in active listening in our relationships is essential, especially when there is conflict. The first step in resolving conflict is for each person to feel heard and understood. In fact, if you can achieve this, you will resolve a great deal of conflict right away. Unfortunately, most people do not do this and it is why they get louder and louder, to the point of yelling at each other. Yelling and screaming happens because in most cases people do not feel heard or understood. In order to be heard, they yell at the other person. If one could stop and really work at hearing the other person, they wouldn't have to yell in order to be understood.

One of the reasons we don't listen is because we really want to make our point. As the other person is speaking, we are thinking about what we will say next that supports why we are right and they are wrong. Guess what? The other person is doing the same thing. So around and around we go, and all we are doing is debating and not resolving anything.

Another reason for not listening well is because we often defend ourselves. If the other person directs an accusation at us, we'll defend ourselves instead of listening to what the person is trying to say. If the other person says something we believe is factually incorrect, we'll defend ourselves by showing them they're wrong. Once again, the end result is we never hear each other and the conflict is never resolved, but being perpetuated and damaging our relationships.

During the many years of pastoral counseling with couples having marital challenges, I would sometimes think to myself, "I wish the Lord would come down and tell me who is right and who is wrong." Of course, that never happened. But I discovered knowing who was right or wrong didn't make a difference. Instead, I came to realize the most important thing was that each person felt heard and understood. I also realized that in the mind of each person who thinks they are right, this is their reality and the other person must deal with their reality. The reverse is true as well. In other words, each person must deal with the other from his or her *perspective* of reality instead of reality itself. Proving someone is wrong leads to conflict, but practicing active listening will help you to understand his or her view of reality, which is the view that must be dealt with. When this happens, the other person feels heard and becomes more open to hearing your view of reality to the point of possibly even changing their mind. This won't happen during a debate where one tries to win and prevail. When you give up trying to be right, to prevail; you have breakthroughs of understanding which will change the climate and make conflict resolution possible.

This is why active listening is vital to conflict resolution. When someone truly feels heard and understood, they no longer need to raise their voice because they are being heard. Active listening and sending "10-4" messages help to break the cycle of conflict.

Another reason people resist using active listening is because they're afraid if they listen closely to the other person and repeat back what they are hearing, the other person will think they're agreeing with them. This is not the case. Just because you hear the other person doesn't mean you agree with them, but only that you've heard them. In fact, after you've sufficiently done active listening, you will have your opportunity to make clear you do not agree – but since you've listened, they'll be more inclined to listen to you and they will know clearly you do not agree.

Years ago, I served in a church that had an elementary school. I was the superintendent, overseeing the work of the school's principal. There was an after-school daycare program that was open until 6 pm for parents who worked. One evening, when the school and church offices were closed, I was working in my office when I heard a pounding at the door. I unlocked the door, only to encounter a very angry father. His anger stemmed from his daughter contracting head lice twice from using the hats at the after-school program. He explained how he had to spend a lot of money buying special anti-lice shampoos to eradicate the lice, and he had met with the after-school director and the principal, asking them to make sure his daughter did not wear the hats. They said they would take care of the problem. Now he was in my office, very angry, because when he arrived to pick up his daughter, she was wearing one of those hats. I listened to everything he said, and then I gave him a "10-4 message." I repeated back to him the basics of what he had told me, saying, "Your daughter gets head lice every time because she uses one of those hats in the after-school program and it is giving her lice... this is costing you a lot of money...you have told the director and the principal, and nothing ever seems to change, and you are very upset over this." Immediately, his temper began to cool and he was able to lower his voice. I told him I would look into the matter and get back to him.

In this moment of conflict, I used active listening to begin the process of resolution. I could have become defensive. I could have said, "Well, you know, there are a great many children in the after-school program; how in the world can our staff possibly keep an eye on your daughter and those hats? Perhaps you should try to teach your daughter not to use these hats and then your problem would be solved. You know our principal is very busy and I'm sure she's doing the best she can." I may have been right to say these things, but the conflict would have become worse. Because I used active listening and gave him the "10-4" message, the father apologized to me for getting so upset. What made the difference is he felt someone understood and heard him. When we do this in our relationships, the temperature comes down and the volume is reduced; now you have the foundation for a resolution to the conflict.

Another way to do active listening is to ask the other person questions. Using this model is almost like being a reporter for a news venue. Reporters are taught to ask Who, What, Where, When, Why and How. When we ask those kinds of questions, even when it's not in a moment of conflict, it shows we are growing in active listening. When we ask questions, we are encouraging the other person to talk and share, and this improves any relationship. However, we do have to be careful in how we use questions in the context of active listening. What is our motive in asking certain questions? If we ask questions that make our point or show that the other person is wrong, we are not doing active listening but rather defending ourselves or trying to win the debate.

To give you an example, one person says, "My boss is terrible because she always questions what I do." The other person responds by asking, "Have you told her this is annoying to you?" While this is a valid question, it is a question with an agenda. The agenda is to try to force the other person to solve the problem; it is not a question which strives to learn more and care about the other. Rather, it is a question that seeks to fix the other person's problem. We may not realize we are doing this, but we are basically saying we are smarter than the other person, we know more, and if the other person would only listen to us, they would be better off. This is not active listening, but an attempt to fix the other person. A better answer would be, "What does it do to you when your boss questions what you do?" This kind of question is an attempt to learn more, and not solve the other person's problem. It is a better way of offering care to them.

Now we are ready, after adequate listening and mutual understanding, to go to the next step which is starting the conflict resolution process. As stated earlier, one test to see if either of you are ready for this step is to ask the other person if they felt you have heard them. If the answer is no, then it means you need to keep listening and reporting back what you have heard. Otherwise, until each of you feels you were heard, it will be difficult to resolve conflict. When each of you reaches the point of saying you have felt heard and understood, you can move to conflict resolution. This next step is called a "win-win solution."

In a win-win solution, you sometimes need to become creative and think outside the box. Because of the active listening you've done, you already understand what is important to the other person. This needs to be taken seriously while you craft a win-win solution. Previously, when the disagreement turned to a debate or a yelling match, you were creating a win-lose situation. One person won, and the other person lost. When that happened, a great deal of bitterness was created. When win-lose situations are the consistent results of these conflicts, they will always damage our relationship.

So what does a win-win solution look like?

Let's say a married couple has an issue over the need for a new refrigerator. Their refrigerator is old and many functions are not working. The icemaker died and drawers are broken. The wife wants a new refrigerator because the couple has family coming to visit this summer. The husband realizes, because of active listening, the old refrigerator isn't working well and he is open to a change. But here's the rub. He doesn't want to go into credit card debt to buy a new refrigerator, and they do not have enough money in their checking account to simply write a check for a new refrigerator. What can they do? What decision can they make to turn this into a win-win solution? One solution could be to find an appliance store which offers interest-free purchases for the first year. As long as it is paid off before the year is over, there is no interest. Another solution shows they have several months before the relatives come to visit, and they could save money to buy the floor model, which would be cheaper. Or they could check Craigslist for one that is only a year or two old at a much-reduced cost.

To create a win-win solution, you need to really listen to each other and think creatively so you can find solutions that work for both of you. This is difficult to do, which is why we don't do it very often in the midst of a conflict. It's easier for the dominant person to not listen and simply announce how things are going to be. The problem with this is the other person is wounded, buries their feelings and becomes increasingly bitter over time.

Sometimes, the difficulties in creating win-win situations stem from our families of origin. We are taught in our families how to make decisions within the context of marriage and family. If you come from a family where one parent was the decision-maker, you and your siblings will often go into your marriages with that model in mind and live it out. If you come from a family where decisions were made through negotiations and win-win solutions, you will expect decisions to be made in that manner. If you have one spouse from a family where one parent made all the decisions; and the other spouse from a family where decisions were negotiated, you have the formula for constant conflict. Conflict is far less likely when both parties come from families where the decision-making model is the same. Think about the decision-making process in your family of origin. If it's different from your spouse's family, this is an insight into the problem, and you both need to create a win-win solution on what model you will use going forward.

Getting to a win-win solution requires active listening and the desire to understand the other before being understood. It means being able to give up trying to convince the other you're right and the other is wrong. It means not trying to defend yourself, but to truly understand the other. At this level, you can even test the situation by asking the other, before it is your turn; to speak and ask them if they feel heard and understood. If the answer is yes, you can move on and share your "view of reality." However, if the answer is no, then you must ask more questions and listen again, giving "10-4 messages" of what you are hearing and reporting back what you have heard. In this way you will be clearer. Then, as you have both listened without defending yourselves, you can move on to the win-win solution. You will have to use your imaginations and do mutual brainstorming in finding a solution that can work for both of you. This can be tested as well, because when you arrive at the solution, you can ask each other whether it was a win-win for them and they can ask the same of you. If the other person says no, it was not a win-win for them, then it is back to the drawing board to find a win-win solution. It may well require more active listening to better understand the other's view of reality.

To be honest, this takes work. It is difficult to do at first because most people were never taught to do this. So many of us come from families where we really don't listen and then try to convince others we are right, and then the table is flipped where the other side does the same. This is the most often used method and the one which fails the most often. When you offer active listening and create win-win solutions, you find significant improvement. However, it means you have to be disciplined in this effort and work at it.

This method in the Language of the Heart will work in every relationship. You can use it with colleagues at work. It will even help in your relationship with your boss. Many parents have found this to be extremely beneficial with their children. Young people, especially adolescents, are going through such challenging times of development and maturation, and it is essential parents, teachers and others practice giving "10-4 messages" to them. Often young people feel isolated, but when someone offers sincere active listening, it gives them real hope. In the Language of the Heart, we do not suggest you offer win-win solutions with teens because the parent always needs to be the parent. But when you do active listening with young people, they will feel heard and be far more compliant with parental expectations and authority. Active listening that is devoid of self-defense, moving toward win-win solutions, will change the climate and find resolution in adult relationships.

CHAPTER FOUR
PUTTING LANGUAGE OF THE HEART INTO ACTION

As I introduced the concept of the Language of the Heart one weekend at church, I showed a fictitious video of a woman with a nail in her forehead. The nail didn't seem to bother the woman. In fact, she didn't even seem to notice it. But her husband did notice it. Whatever she said did not matter because he was focused on the nail in her forehead. He started making subtle attempts to address the issue, but she kept talking over his attempts. All he wanted to do was to deal with the nail in his wife's forehead and solve her problem. All she wanted was to talk. This was a great way to illustrate one of the major problems when people try to communicate.

Have you ever had a relationship like that? Not one with someone having a nail in their forehead of course, but a relationship where one wants to be heard and the other wants to solve the other's problems. This happens a great deal in all of our relationships, where one person shares their heart and the other person is trying to fix the other's perceived problem. It is especially prevalent within marriages.

MORE THAN A FEELING

In previous chapters, we have come to understand the Language of the Heart is the ability to have feelings and emotions, and the ability to allow others to have their emotions. We have learned that our job in most relationships is not to solve the other person's problems, but rather to be a good listener and try to understand. Within the context of the Language of the Heart, I call this being a "care-giver." A "care-taker" tries to solve the other person's problems, but a care-giver just listens and tries to understand. One of the ways we can do this effectively is to use the active listening methods discussed earlier. Remember, active listening is basically reporting back what you have heard the other person say. You don't defend yourself or try to convince the other why they are wrong. You let them have their say, and report back what you have heard. Just because you listen to someone doesn't mean you agree with him or her. It only means you have heard and understood them. In the Language of the Heart, we listen and remain calm, not defending ourselves. We are to be the "non-anxious presence in an anxious moment." After you do this, it's your turn to be heard and to share your thoughts.

If you were to do just that, you would improve every relationship in your life. By being a care-giver and listening to the other, you will be amazed at the positive changes made by taking these steps, and if both of you are doing this for each other, it will turbo-charge your relationship.

Remember too, another aspect of the Language of the Heart is the ability to have and experience your emotions. It is the ability to identify and even articulate those emotions, and the ability to listen to others as they share their emotions without saying, "I know how you feel" or "You shouldn't feel that way." All feelings are legitimate, and we allow the other person to have ownership of their feelings without trying to talk them out of having them. If you try to talk them out of their feelings, it is care-taking instead of care-giving. It is trying to solve the other person's problem without really listening to them...it is like trying to take the nail out of their forehead.

I'm absolutely convinced one of the greatest problems in relationships is we don't listen to each other deeply enough. Instead, we expend effort in trying to fix others and solving their problems, or defending ourselves. We are very uncomfortable with people having emotions, so we try to patch them up, talk them out of the feelings so they are "stable" again. What many do not understand is the ability to have emotions in the long term is what keeps people stable, because God created us to have emotions as coping mechanisms for the challenges and setbacks life throws at us.

So the Language of the Heart is the ability to have feelings and emotions, and the ability to listen to other people's feelings and emotions without trying to fix them. As important as this definition is, the Language of the Heart goes much deeper. It is more than feelings. At its very foundation, the Language of the Heart is really about *our HEARTS*. It is about the need for our hearts to be changed by the grace of God in Jesus Christ. When the unconditional love of God pours into our hearts through a relationship with Jesus, we have *a change of heart*. Religion will not give this to you. Only a relationship with Jesus will give this to you. When He changes our hearts with His love, we are better able to love others as He loves them.

IT IS WHAT COMES OUT OF OUR HEART THAT MATTERS

One day, Jesus was confronted by the religious leaders and was asked about the conduct of His disciples. It seemed that there were some religious rules they weren't following. According to the religious traditions, they were supposed to wash their hands for spiritual purity before they ate, and they weren't doing this. The religious leaders were condemning Jesus and His disciples, and Jesus fired back at the religious leaders; sharing a short parable of explanation with His disciples. He made the point that all these religious leaders were concerned about was outward spirituality and appearances. Then one of the disciples asked Jesus what He meant and He said the following:

"Do you not see that whatever goes into the mouth enters the stomach, and goes out into the sewer? But what comes out of the mouth proceeds from the heart, and this is what defiles. For out of the heart come evil intentions, murder, adultery, fornication, theft, false witness, slander. These are what defile a person, but to eat with unwashed hands does not defile."
– Matthew 15:17-20

The key to spiritual growth is for our hearts to be changed and transformed. We can appear to be many things, and profess many things. We can produce many spiritual practices, but at the end of the day, the only thing that matters is our heart. It is what comes out of us that matters. It is what is within our core, and over time, will show through the outer veneer of spirituality, sophistication, education, power, or anything else we use to appear to "have it all together." It is our heart that matters. We will never truly be able to practice the Language of the Heart unless our heart changes.

By that, I mean we all have a bad heart because of our sinful nature. And out of this heart comes many things that destroy or damage the relationships in our lives. We lie, we use power inappropriately, sometimes we are immoral; and all of this comes out of our hearts. One of the greatest problems of our heart is our pride and arrogance.

PRIDE & ARROGANCE ARE SERIOUS ROADBLOCKS TO HEALTHY RELATIONSHIPS

There is a very serious sin that in my estimation is doing a great deal of harm, holding back revival, destroying homes, and causing Christians to live in failure and defeat. Very frankly, it is the sin of pride.

Pride is such a deceitful sin. I heard a pastor say, "Many people who are infected and infested with pride have no idea that they are. As a matter of fact, the proud person is often very proud of his humility."

What is pride? Pride is thinking we are self-reliant and self-sufficient. Pride says we don't really need anyone else, maybe not even God. Pride is also esteeming one's self above other people. Do you think that because you have achieved certain things or have certain possessions you're better than somebody else?

Here are some of the indications of a proud person:

- We have a very difficult time admitting mistakes and saying, "I am wrong."
- We don't have a teachable spirit because we already know everything.
- We accept praise for things we haven't done.
- We want things done our way, to the point of "my way or the highway."
- We demand things be done our way because that's the only way it can be done.
- We often use power inappropriately at home and at work.
- We believe we are the smartest person in the room.

Every relationship is affected negatively because of pride. Many times you can see the effect of pride in our lives by how many friendships we have. Do our adult children want relationships with us, or did they move out of our home as quickly as they could? When we are filled with pride and have climbed the corporate ladder or amassed a fortune, our colleagues do not esteem us but avoid us.

In Proverbs 11:2, we read:

"When pride comes, then comes disgrace; but wisdom is with the humble."

PRIDE DESTROYS, HOWEVER, HUMILITY IS THE LANGUAGE OF THE HEART

One of the fundamental reasons we struggle with living out the Language of the Heart is because our hearts are full of pride, which makes it almost impossible to learn the Language of the

Heart. We must give up our pride, and in a moment I'll tell you how you can do just that.

The other obstacle to learning the Language of the Heart are the wounds of our lives. Dr. Ed Ewart serves on the staff of our church as a pastor with many much-appreciated years of experience. Out of those years of experience, he has summarized something of tremendous depth and wisdom for me. Pastor Ed has said from time to time, "Hurt people hurt people." Often this is what happens in our lives. When we have been hurt, it can cause us to lash out and hurt other people, and often we don't even know we are doing this. This hurt could have been caused by the death of someone fundamental to our lives when we were children, or by abuse, or when we were left by someone in a divorce, or fired from a job. It can be any number of things, but we walk around with this hurt and these wounds, and we hurt others with our hurt without even realizing it. Hurt people hurt people. When you hook that up with pride, you have a toxic mix that damages many of our relationships and prevents us from learning the biblical principles of the Language of the Heart, which can heal these relationships and prevent dysfunction.

Additionally, because of past wounds, some people act out their wounds in terms of some form of addiction. Whether it is an addiction to drugs, alcohol or anything else; it adds dysfunction to our lives. Even though we still don't know the cause of addiction, whether genetic or a learned trait, or both, it is still destructive to our lives. Once again, when we hook up pride with addiction we have another toxic mix. Most addicts I have known are in denial about their problem and often this is due to pride. Some of their family members enable them, and as a result, a family is in crisis. Some families are in crisis for years and for multiple generations, when the cycle of addiction is not broken. Sometimes an intervention with a professional counselor is needed to break the cycle and get the help is needed for the addict and the family. Treatment for the addict is the only way to change the situation. A Christian counselor is also helpful in helping other family members to learn to put the pieces back together. Counseling can help you heal the hurt that causes you to hurt others. But the point is pride and arrogance are part of the mix and brings great pain and destruction.

GRACE IS THE ANSWER

So what is the answer? What can we do about this problem of pride and hurt that causes us to be toxic to those around us? *The answer is called* **grace!**

In Matthew 18, Jesus told a parable about a king who wanted to settle accounts with those who owed him money. One of the first men brought to him owed him 10,000 talents, which is equivalent to millions of dollars today. In other words, it was a debt that was impossible to pay. When the man could not pay the king, the king ordered that the man, his wife, and his children be sold into slavery and the money would be used to pay his debt. Theologian and writer, Dr. Frederick Dale Bruner[3] points out in his commentary something interesting in this story about how big everything is. The man owed the kind of debt no one would ever be able to pay. And to sell the man's wife and children was against Jewish law, which only points to the fact there was no way the man could pay the debt – he did not have the resources to pay the impossible debt. The man would have needed countless lives to be able to pay the debt – it was that enormous.

This man was not very concerned about this debt until he was confronted with the debt. This happens to us because of our pride. We don't recognize we have a tremendous debt because of our sin and it is beyond anything we can pay to God. Yet, in our pride, we go on as if everything is just fine.

But then this man, realizing his hopeless and helpless condition, fell on his knees and begged for mercy, and the king granted it to him. Then what happened next is amazing. As he left the king's presence, he bumped into someone who owed him money – let's say about $3,000 – and he demanded payment. When the man could not pay him, he had the man put into prison. Imagine this – he was forgiven many millions of dollars of debt and let out of prison, but the man who owed him significantly less was put into prison.

"When his fellow slaves saw what had happened, they were greatly distressed, and they went and reported to their lord all that had taken place. Then his lord summoned him and said to him, 'You wicked slave! I forgave you all that debt because you pleaded with me. Should you not have had mercy on your fellow slave, as I had mercy on you?' And in anger, his lord handed him over to be tortured until he would pay his entire debt. So my heavenly Father will also do to every one of you, if you do not forgive your brother or sister from your heart." – Matthew 18:31-35

What went wrong? The man experienced grace but would

not give grace to anyone else! This parable is a picture of someone who receives grace, or in this case the forgiveness of God, but will not give it to another. Grace is also God's love and unmerited favor. The foundation of the Language of the Heart is to learn how to give the grace we have received.

THE LANGUAGE OF THE HEART IS TO GIVE AWAY THE GRACE YOU HAVE RECEIVED

What we see in this man in the parable is pride and arrogance on display. This is an example of pride and how "hurt people hurt people." What is needed is a changed heart. In fact, a heart transplant is needed. And through Jesus Christ, that is what God offers you today. Think of God as the heart surgeon, cracking open your chest, removing your heart – as poisoned as it is with pride and pain – and replacing it with his own heart through Jesus Christ. Rather than telling you to change, He creates the change. Do you clean up so He can accept you? No, He accepts you and begins cleaning you up. His dream isn't just to get you into heaven, but to get heaven into you. What a difference this makes! Can't forgive your enemy? Can't face tomorrow? Can't forgive your past? Christ can, and He is on the move, aggressively budging you from a graceless life to grace-shaped living.

HEALING THE WOUNDS OF WAR: THE KIM PHUC STORY

There is an iconic photograph that comes out of the Vietnam War. It is photograph of a young girl by the name of Phan Thi

Kim Phuc. On June 8, 1972, a napalm bomb was dropped on her village, and Kim, who was just nine years old, went running from her hiding place naked with her arms outstretched and with skin flapping from her legs. She cried out, "Nong qua! Nong qua!" which means, "Too hot! Too hot!" I can only imagine the terror and pain that she experienced. Ruth Schenk[4] goes on to tell us what happened next. Ruth reports the following:

Doctors said Kim would never survive, but after 14 months in the hospital – and 17 surgeries – she returned to her family. However, despite her physical recovery, Kim was seldom free from pain, nightmares and anger.

As Kim tells her story, she says, "The anger inside me was like a hatred high as a mountain, and my bitterness was black as old coffee. I hated my life. I hated all people who were normal, because I was not normal. I wanted to die many times. Doctors helped heal my wounds, but they couldn't heal my heart."

Then Kim found a bible while spending time in a library. It confused her because it was different than her religion, but her brother-in-law had a friend who was a Christian. She arranged to see him with her list of questions, and after they talked, this friend invited Kim to visit his church for a Christmas service. The end of the service was a turning point in Kim's life after 10 years of pain.

"I could not wait to trust the Lord," Kim said. "[Jesus] helped me learn to forgive my enemies, and I finally had some peace in my heart."

Since that time, Kim has actually met the man who ordered

the bombing and they have found reconciliation. She has written books and is an active Christian speaker. All because she has given to others the grace she has received. The Language of the Heart is to give away the grace you have received.

The only way you can learn the Language of the Heart is to know and experience God's grace through Jesus Christ. We have to let go of our pride because, as one theologian has said, "Grace and pride are antithetical." Only when we experience and live grace will we have the teachable spirit necessary for learning the Language of the Heart. Only when we experience grace can we find the healing for the hurt that causes us to hurt other people.

You need to say to Jesus, "I have been filled with pride and hurt, and I need Your forgiveness and grace. I give You my very life – You take over and heal me, then I can begin to learn the Language of the Heart."

Then:

- You can learn to listen to others.
- You can learn how to share your own emotion and your own pain.
- You can learn to be brave and come out of the shadows of not saying anything and swallowing your pain.
- You can learn to listen to others.

Grace gives you the power to be brave, to speak, and forgive others.

CHAPTER FIVE
THINKING BEFORE WE SPEAK

We have learned that the Language of the Heart is the ability to feel feelings and emotions, and the emotion of others, and then to build bridges of reconciliation. Basically, it is learning to love others as God loves other people. There are many things that get in the way of doing this. We realize that pride and arrogance often get in the way; our hubris gets in the way of relating well with people. To practice the Language of the Heart, we need to set our arrogance aside and become servants to others in our lives. When we become servants in how we treat others, we will be doing what Jesus did, and we will improve every relationship. Let's examine this new aspect of growing in the Language of the Heart.

LACK OF SELF-CONTROL WILL DAMAGE YOUR RELATIONSHIPS

Another aspect of the Language of the Heart has to do with the ability to control our reactions to others and to have filters as we speak to them. There are many examples in the Bible of people who could not control themselves. These were people who were impulsive, reactive, and not able to exercise self-control. They exploded and wondered why people didn't want to have relationships with them.

In the story of the Prodigal Son in Luke Chapter 15, we find just such an example. This young man goes to his father and asks for his entire inheritance, which is granted to him. The young man goes off and lives a wild life as a party animal, spending his money on decadent and immoral living. When he runs out of money, he finds himself eating with the pigs and realizes that the servants in his father's house have it better than he, and perhaps his father would take him back as a servant. He begins his journey home to beg for help. The Bible says when the young man's father (the father is a picture of God) sees him at a distance, he runs to him and embraces him, and orders a party to be thrown for him, because he was dead and was now alive. While the party is going on, the Prodigal Son's older brother shows up, and look at what happens next:

"Now his elder son was in the field; and when he came and approached the house, he heard music and dancing. He called one of the slaves and asked what was going on. He replied, 'Your brother has come, and your father has killed the fatted calf, because he has got him back safe and sound.' Then he became angry and refused to go in. His father came out and began to plead with him. But he answered his father, 'Listen! For all these years I have been working like a slave for you, and I have never disobeyed your command; yet you have never given me even a young goat so that I might celebrate with my friends. But when this son of yours came

back, who has devoured your property with prostitutes, you killed the fatted calf for him!' Then the father said to him, 'Son, you are always with me, and all that is mine is yours. But we had to celebrate and rejoice, because this brother of yours was dead and has come to life; he was lost and has been found.'"– Luke 15:25-32

This older brother reacts with a lack of fluency in the Language of the Heart. Instead of rejoicing and being glad that his younger brother is home and safe, he is filled with pride and indignation. He calls his younger brother "this son of yours," not "my brother." He does not love as God loves. He won't go into the party. His father comes out and pleads with him to join the party, and he says, "Look, I've been working for you like a slave – *not a son, but a slave* – all these years and you have never given me a party." The father says to him, "You are always with me and all that I have is yours." What is the older brother doing? He is thinking and acting like a *victim*.

"Victimspeak" is when we say things like "I am not appreciated around here" or "no one cares about me" or "they don't recognize my contributions." In victimspeak you are saying, "Please feel sorry for me because I am so empty inside that this is the only way I can feel whole – by you feeling sorry for me."

If you need to know if you speak and act like a victim, you can test this by asking those in your life who know you best. Ask these people if you use key phrases like the ones mentioned above. If they tell you that you do speak and act like a victim, try to have a teachable spirit and allow that insight to help you grow. In the Language of the Heart, you give up being the victim and find your worth in God's love through Jesus Christ. Then you are able to rejoice and celebrate when good things happen to other people, regardless of their circumstances. This is what the older brother in the story could not do. He was unable to rejoice that his younger brother was home and restored. He saw himself as a victim and that's where he was stuck. When we think and react like victims, we need to change. When we reflect on the sacrifice that God made for us in the cross of Jesus, we come to know that we are of great value. The fact that Jesus would die for you means you are not a victim, but a child of God, and you now can rejoice in God blessing and restoring someone else.

The older brother has no filter and just reacts out of his own pain; his reaction does not strengthen his relationship with his family. One of the important aspects of the Language of the Heart is to have greater clarity about why we say what we say. When we understand where our harsh words come from, we will be able to think before we speak, and place boundaries around our words and ideas that we share with others. Learning this might require sessions with a Christian therapist, who can help you explore why you say what you say.

The story of John and James, the "Sons of Thunder," is another example of the inability to think before speaking. In Mark Chapter 3, we read about how Jesus was calling His twelve disciples. Among the first to be called by Jesus were James and John, brothers and the sons of Zebedee. Jesus gave them a nickname – "Sons of Thunder." Why would He call them that?

Some have speculated that Jesus saw their future boldness of preaching the gospel. But it could also have something to do with the time in Luke Chapter 9, when Jesus and His disciples entered a Samaritan town and the people didn't receive Jesus because, as Luke said, "His face was set toward Jerusalem," which meant that He was preparing for the Cross. Since they wouldn't receive Jesus, James and John asked, "Jesus, would you like us to pray for fire to come down from heaven and destroy this village and all of its people?" The Bible says Jesus rebuked them, and this might be the reason for their nicknames – because they would just say whatever came to their minds. They didn't think before they spoke. But wait, it only gets better.

In Mark Chapter 10, Jesus and the disciples are going up to Jerusalem and He takes them aside, and tells them what will soon happen to Him. He explains that He will be handed over to the chief priests and scribes, and they will condemn Him to death. He goes on to explain that He will be tortured by the Gentiles and killed, but that after three days He will rise from the dead. Now look at how James and John respond to this powerful proclamation of Jesus:

"James and John, the sons of Zebedee, came forward to Him and said to Him, "Teacher, we want You to do for us whatever we ask of You." And He said to them, "What is it You want me to do for you?" And they said to Him, "Grant us to sit, one at Your right hand and one at Your left, in Your glory." But Jesus said to them, "You do not know what you are asking. Are you able to drink the cup that I drink, or be baptized with the baptism that I am baptized with?" They

replied, "We are able." Then Jesus said to them, "The cup that I drink you will drink; and with the baptism with which I am baptized, you will be baptized; but to sit at My right hand or at My left is not Mine to grant, but it is for those for whom it has been prepared." When the ten heard this, they began to be angry with James and John." – Mark 10:35-41

After Jesus shares with His disciples His entire mission for coming to earth, He explains the pain and suffering He will undergo. James and John ask if they can sit at His right and left hands when He enters His kingdom. In other words, it's all about them. It's their needs and wants that must be considered. All they can think about is what they want, and not the greater picture.

It gets worse because the way that Matthew remembers it. In Matthew Chapter 20, it is the *mother* of James and John who asks on their behalf. The problem is systemic in the entire family. In the next verses, Jesus would instruct them to learn how to forget themselves and to die to themselves, and learn how to be servants. Had James and John been fluent in the Language of the Heart, they would have thought about what they were saying before they said it. They would have had a filter for what they said, and would have given consideration to Jesus. They would have thought first about what Jesus had said and responded within that context.

James and John were acting like our children. When parents speak to their children about the need to move because of a job loss, or they've found a job they need to take in another area, the children say, "But what about my friends?" That's okay because they are children, but when adults do it, they are showing that they aren't fluent in the Language of the Heart. They are just thinking about themselves and being consumed with themselves. With the Language of the Heart, you discover the love of God through Jesus, which causes you to want to forget yourself and serve others. In relationships, having a servant's heart and putting others ahead of yourself strengthens every relationship.

THE LANGUAGE OF THE HEART TEACHES US TO RESPECT AND SERVE EVERYONE AROUND US

The Language of the Heart teaches us, through Biblical principles, we do not just say whatever comes to mind. We have filters that we use to process our thoughts before we speak. We ask ourselves if what we are about to say is loving and kind. We ask ourselves if our speech will build the other person up or tear them down. It is essential that we think before we speak.

The Book of Genesis provides a wonderful example of this in the form of a very dysfunctional family. Jacob was the father to several sons. The problem was that the older sons were very jealous of their youngest brother, Joseph, because their father, Jacob, had a real fondness for this son of his old age. In their jealousy, the brothers sold Joseph to some travelers. They went back to their father and told him Joseph had been killed by animals; showing him Joseph's many-colored coat covered with blood. Jacob didn't know that not only was Joseph alive, but in the years to come Joseph would rise to prominence in the land of Egypt, being put in charge of the agricultural department, saving the people from starvation. There was a famine throughout the region and finally Jacob told his sons to go to Egypt to see if they could obtain some food, which they did. This put them in direct contact with their brother, Joseph. They didn't recognize him but he recognized them. What is so fascinating about Joseph is that he didn't want vengeance, but instead, reconciliation. He gave them food and asked them about their family, especially their father. Then he revealed himself and they were afraid. Look at what Joseph said to them on two different occasions:

"Then Joseph said to his brothers, "Come closer to me." And they came closer. He said, "I am your brother, Joseph, whom you sold into Egypt. And now do not be distressed, or angry with yourselves, because you sold me here; for God sent me before you to preserve life." – Genesis 45:4-5

"But Joseph said to them, "Do not be afraid! Am I in the place of God? Even though you intended to do harm to me, God intended it for good, in order to preserve a numerous people, as He is doing today. So have no fear; I myself will provide for you and your little ones." In this way he reassured them, speaking kindly to them."
– Genesis 50:19-21

Joseph spoke the Language of the Heart and his brothers did not. They were filled with hatred and jealousy toward Joseph when they were young. Now, they were concerned they would be punished, and that Joseph would have vengeance upon them because that was what they would have done.

On the other hand, Joseph wanted the best for his brothers. He wanted to be restored to his father, which eventually happened. Joseph spoke the Language of the Heart and could see God's hand in the entire situation. He knew God's love and wasn't jealous of anyone. He could see the big picture and understood how God could take this bad situation and turn it into something good. He looked at life through the eyes of faith and trust in God, not in himself.

This is the Language of the Heart, knowing God's love in such a way that you are not jealous of others, nor seeking vengeance; but rather reconciliation. You don't need vengeance or jealousy because you have experienced the love of God in Jesus Christ. His love is the Language of the Heart, as you will learn to love others as He loves them.

SELF-CONTROL

What we see missing in these stories of the Prodigal Son's older brother, the Sons of Thunder James and John and their mother; is the ability to have self-control. In Galatians Chapter 5, Paul speaks of the fruit of the Spirit, which again is the Language of the Heart. The last one listed is the flavor of self-control:

"By contrast, the fruit of the Spirit is love, joy, peace, patience, kindness, generosity, faithfulness, gentleness, and self-control." – Galatians 5:22-23a

If you want to improve the relationships in your life, learn to practice self-control. *We need to think before we speak.* There are people who say whatever they feel like saying, whenever they feel like saying it. Some are even proud of this, and sometimes say, "I speak my mind." The problem is that speaking their mind often hurts other people. It might be the reason they have few friends and their adult children don't want much to do with them.

Instead, in the Language of the Heart, we teach that to improve our relationships we must use our words carefully. Think about what you say before you say it. Before you speak, instill a self-filter that asks:

- Would this be kind and loving?
- Am I using power responsibly? Is this an inappropriate use of power?
- Will it build them up or tear them down?
- Will what I am going to say enhance my pride, or help me be a servant?
- Am I being jealous, vengeful or being a victim?
- Am I being selfish?

Start thinking before you speak. Practice self-control and have a filter – and then speak the Language of the Heart by loving other people as God loves them...because then you will be improving every relationship you have.

CHAPTER SIX
THE VALUE OF A TEACHABLE SPIRIT

Once we have had emotional and spiritual heart replacement surgery, we can genuinely begin to grow in our ability to speak this foreign language called the Language of the Heart. We are now in a better position to be taught. Our pride is being removed and we have a teachable spirit.

Many of us have lives headed for problems and difficulties. Others have tried to tell us to change or take a different course, and we ignore them. We laugh at them and think that they are ridiculous and wrong. However, we're the ones who end up being damaged. The Language of the Heart is able to help us grow and be in better places, but it says that we need to have "a teachable spirit."

THE ECHO CHAMBER OF OUR OWN IDEAS

The ability to take advice and learn from others is another part of the Language of the Heart. In order for us to learn any of the skills required by the Language of the Heart, we need to be open to being taught. Too often, this is where many people fail in their relationships – they are going to do what they want to do no matter what. The only person they listen to is themselves because they believe they're right. Often, in arguments and disagreements, the person lacking in a teachable spirit has one goal – to prove themselves right and others wrong. If they can convince you that they are right (which, of course, they are) and you are wrong (which, of course, you are), then everything will be just fine. Then, of course, there is an argument, and it all stems from an unteachable spirit.

It has been said of such people, "Don't confuse them with facts; their minds are made up." This is the description of a single-minded stubborn person. Successful relationships demand there be a give and take, where each person respects and even honors the other person. When this doesn't happen, it damages the relationship because someone is bound to feel diminished, shamed and oppressed.

Kelly Clarkson sings of what happens when relationships like this end. "Since you've been gone, I can breathe for the first time."[5] When you're in a relationship with someone who lacks a teachable spirit, you often feel like you can't breathe, you walk on eggshells, and you have to be very careful in what you say and do. The result is an unhealthy relationship. If you try to make suggestions, you're met with a brick wall because there isn't much give and take. Rarely is there a win-win solution to the problem. Most of the time it's a win-lose situation; they win and you lose.

When you lack a teachable spirit, you only hear your own voice. Have you ever been on the edge of a cliff or in a cave and heard your own voice? "Hello...hello...hello...hello..." "Is anybody there...is anybody there...is anybody there..." You didn't hear someone else; you heard only yourself. You heard the echo of your own voice. This same effect can be produced electronically in a recording studio, in what is called an echo chamber. So when we lack a teachable spirit, we are living in a type of echo chamber. I call it the Echo Chamber Effect.

With the Echo Chamber Effect, you only hear your own voice, your own thoughts and your own ideas. Unless you are the brightest person ever, you'll remain stuck where you are and you won't grow. Nothing will really improve in your life because you listen only to yourself. However, God has a better way for us to live our lives.

THE NEED FOR A TEACHABLE SPIRIT

In Psalm 81, God laments and grieves that His people would not listen to Him. He laments that they have turned to other gods and have pushed Him away from helping them. Then, in verses 11-16, God continues to speak to His people, then and now. He speaks to those of us who live with the Echo Chamber Effect.

"But My people did not listen to My voice; Israel would not submit to Me. So I gave them over to their stubborn hearts, to follow their own counsels. O that My people would listen to Me, that Israel would walk in My ways! Then I would quickly subdue their enemies, and turn My hand against their foes. Those who hate the LORD would cringe before Him, and their doom would last forever. I would feed you with the finest of the wheat, and with honey from the rock I would satisfy

God says when we have an un-teachable spirit, He steps back from us and says, "Okay, you handle it. I will allow you to have your stubborn heart." In other words, God says, "I will allow you to live in your echo chamber." The result is that our lives become a mess as our families are broken, our careers stagnate, and we rarely have deep and lasting friendships. God just leaves us to ourselves and we implode.

He says that if we would have a teachable spirit, He would be able to bless us. We would have the "finest wheat" and the "finest honey" which would satisfy us. There would be blessings in our lives if we have a teachable spirit.

In II Kings 5, there's a story about a man named Naaman. He was in charge of the Army of Aram, which is modern day Syria. Naaman was of high rank, as he was just under the King of Aram (Syria). But he had a problem in the form of a disease. People could see that he had leprosy. On one of his military campaigns, he had taken a girl captive from Israel and had her become the maid to his wife. This maid went to the wife and said she wished Naaman would go to the prophet in Israel so he could be healed. This was passed on to Naaman and he went to the king of Syria, asking if he could go to Israel to be healed. The king agreed and wrote a letter of explanation to the King of Israel. This upset the King of Israel, thinking it was a threat of some kind.

When the Prophet Elisha heard about this, he sent word to the King of Israel that Naaman should be sent to him, and this was done. Naaman, with his entourage of soldiers and horses, went to Elisha's home and the Prophet Elisha sent word to Naaman, through a messenger, that he should go to the River Jordan and wash himself seven times, and then he would be healed.

Now, let's see what happens next:

"But Naaman became angry and went away, saying, "I thought that for me he would surely come out, and stand and call on the name of the LORD his God, and would wave his hand over the spot, and cure the leprosy! Are not Abana and Pharpar, the rivers of Damascus, better than all the waters of Israel? Could I not wash in them, and be clean?" He turned and went away in a rage. But his servants approached and said to him, "Father, if the prophet had commanded you to do something difficult, would you not have done it? How much more, when all he said to you was, 'Wash, and be clean'?" So he went down and immersed himself seven times in the Jordan, according to the word of the man of God; his flesh was restored like the flesh of a young boy, and he was clean."
– II Kings 5:11-14

Notice the attitude Naaman has; an un-teachable spirit. It is an attitude of pride and arrogance. He says, "I thought that for me, he would surely come out of his house but he sends a messenger – doesn't he know who I am? I am a VIP. I am in charge of the Syrian Army and I only answer to the King of Syria." He is used to being honored and revered, and is shocked by how the prophet treats him.

And then he is upset that he must wash in the Jordan. He thought he was superior to the people of Israel. Why does he have to wash in their river, because his homeland is superior to theirs? The arrogance and pride is thick here. And so he was going to go back home because he wasn't being treated the way in which he believes he should be treated. He would just leave and give up on the possibility of being healed because of his pride. Do you see how damaging pride can be?

But the prophet knew what he was doing. He knew that in order for God to heal Naaman, the man would first need to be humble and have a teachable spirit. This is true for us as well. In order for our marriage, family and other relationships to be healed, we must have a teachable spirit.

Finally, when he agreed to wash in the Jordan seven times, he was healed. Had he continued to be proud and unteachable, he would have missed out on being healed. How many times have we missed out on having our relationships healed because we were too proud and had an un-teachable spirit? What great things have we missed because we decided to live in the echo chamber?

Our unteachable spirit prevents us from being able to live out the Language of the Heart. When it has to be "our way or the highway," we aren't easy to be around. Others are nervous and can't relax. We end up offering "law" and not "gospel." However, when we practice the Language of the Heart by being teachable, we are pleasant to be around. We offer grace to others and they enjoy being around us. They stand in line to be our friend while others want to work with us. Someone special wants to be married to us, and stay married to us, and life just has a lot more joy – all because we have a teachable spirit.

Another way in which we lack a teachable spirit is when

we are in denial about an addiction we might be dealing with. In fact, the biggest challenge is the fact that many live in denial about their addictions, which is the same as not having a teachable spirit. In denial, once again, our pride is aflame. When professionals or family members tell us that they believe we have an addiction and we need professional help, we won't listen. A person in denial will say such things as, "I don't have a problem," or "I can quit any time I want." Many times I have heard someone in this situation say that they have it all under control. This is being in denial and nothing in our lives will get better as long as we remain in denial.

This is also true when it comes to marriages. When a wife tells her husband he needs to join her for marital therapy, he will often tell her he is not the one with the problem. But this cannot be true because it takes two to make a marriage work. Again, this is a sign of the lack of a teachable spirit and nothing will get better until we break out of denial. Reach out for professional help with a teachable spirit and you will discover that there is hope for a better day.

When it comes to mental health issues, our pride controls us. Often, because of our pride and the stigma surrounding mental health issues, many people refrain from getting the help they need for themselves and their families. So many times a family will have a member who is clearly demonstrating mental health problems and family members want to keep a lid on the problem, as if to say that if we ignore it, the problem will go away. The only problem is that it will not go away. Then something terrible happens and we are saddened that we did not reach out to a professional for help. What keeps us locked into this cycle of destruction is the lack of a teachable spirit. If you are experiencing these issues, reach out to a professional and get the help you need right away. Don't wait! In addition, if you have loved ones who are suggesting that you need help, listen to them. They are seeing something you may not be able to see for yourself. Be open to receiving help from a doctor or mental health professional and do what they ask. Things really will get better if you do.

Pastor Rick Warren of Saddleback Church has been encouraging churches to push aside the stigma when it comes to mental health issues, so people will reach out to mental health professionals for help. Reaching out to these professionals can be a lifesaver and will help improve relationships.

"Poverty and disgrace are for the one who ignores instruction, but one who heeds reproof is honored."
– Proverbs 13:18

This is a promise from God. If we have a teachable spirit, we will be honored in the relationships in our lives. I realize this is difficult to do. For many, they have been living like this for a long time. It has been such a way of life that we don't always recognize we are doing some of these things, or we have and just say, "Well, you can't teach an old dog new tricks." This is not true.

In his book, *An Anthropologist on Mars*, neurologist Oliver Sacks tells about Virgil, a man who had been blind since early childhood. At the age of 50, Virgil underwent a surgery that restored his sight. In the weeks and months that followed, Dr.

Sacks discovered that just because you have the ability to see physically, it is not the same as seeing.

Virgil's first experiences with sight were difficult for him. While he recognized shapes and colors, he had difficulty organizing what he saw in his brain. He had to re-learn how to see because his behavior was that of someone who was blind. Dr. Sacks said, "One must die as a blind person to be born again as a seeing person. It is the interim, the limbo that is so terrible."[6]

This is how it is to learn many of these biblical principles of the Language of the Heart. At first, they don't seem normal because we have to adjust to them and work at it. Often we need to get help, perhaps from a pastor or a Christian therapist so we can learn to see in new and healthy ways.

So, let's begin to readjust our sight; to go from blindness to greater sight. First, we have to determine if we are living in the echo chamber and are suffering from the Echo Chamber Effect. How do we know if we are doing this? Dr. Marty Williams, a pastor of Family Ministries asks the question we all must ask of ourselves today: "Am I teachable?" He has several thoughts to help us discover if we are teachable:

- I am willing to listen more than to talk.
- I admit when I am mistaken.
- I am able to agree to disagree.
- I desire information more than answers.
- I enjoy asking questions.
- I am open to suggestions and new ideas.
- I feel comfortable asking for advice or directions.
- I can appreciate criticism without being deeply wounded.[7]

Let me add some more questions to go deeper in determining if you have a teachable spirit:

- Am I willing to go to counseling?
- Am I willing to go to A.A. or some other program for addiction if this has been suggested by a counselor?
- Am I willing to take classes in areas of marital improvement or parenting skills, and have an appetite for learning what the class has to offer?
- Am I willing to read books on relationships?
- Do I draw a line in the sand and say I will only do this much spiritually and no more?
- Ask someone who is close to you and knows you well, "Do I have a teachable spirit?"

If it looks like you need to grow in this way, take the steps to grow. Take a class, go to Christian counseling. Ask someone to point out to you when you aren't being teachable. Learn to compromise and strive to find a win-win solution. Any and all of these methods, and many more, will help you to get down the road. The first step is to say to the Lord, "I need a teachable spirit; please give me one and send the people I need to help me learn." Ask the Lord to give you humility to admit when you are wrong and to help you ask more questions and to have a hunger for learning. In these ways you can begin to develop a more teachable spirit and improve every relationship in your life.

CHAPTER SEVEN
THE VALUE OF TRUSTWORTHINESS

We have been making the case that the Language of the Heart is the ability to have feelings and emotions, and the ability to allow others to have their emotions. It is the ability to share and articulate your emotions and feelings to others safely. Earlier, we said in order to learn how to be able to do this, we would need a "heart transplant." Our old heart is filled with pride and selfishness, and needs to be replaced with the very heart of God, and we need to be made into a new creation. When this happens and we give up ownership of our lives to Jesus Christ, we also let go of our pride and arrogance, and have a teachable spirit.

So let's use our teachable spirit to learn other aspects of the Language of the Heart, which would be in the realm of character development. Beyond being able to have and listen to feelings, we need to conduct ourselves in better ways. These character issues are often tied to our pride and ego. When we lack the character required of the Language of the Heart, people do not want to have deep and fulfilling relationships with us. Now, with a new heart and a teachable spirit, let us deal with an important character trait of the Language of the Heart; trustworthiness.

THE BALONEY FACTOR

To make an important point during a sermon I gave, I arranged for one of our members to come out on stage, interrupt me and whisper into my ear. Here's what happened.

Jeff Rogers came out and whispered something into my ear. I looked confused at first, but then audibly said, "Well, I wasn't thinking about you doing that now...but, um...well, all right...go ahead and we'll just see how it goes."

Jeff said, "Okay," and turned to the congregation. "Well, last week, I was really thinking about that video we showed before the message; about the guy who wouldn't listen to his wife, and I was thinking a lot of guys afterward probably realized that they should do that, too. And maybe they were thinking they should do something nice for the beautiful woman they married. My guess is that most of us tend to have the knee jerk reaction of buying flowers, but then I remembered there is something even better than flowers...something no woman will suspect...but that can be a total game changer as a gift; something that can really help you speak the Language of the Heart effectively to her. Now, you probably aren't going to believe this, but it's absolutely true and I challenge you to read about it online. The gift that can totally transform your marriage or relationship and bring you closer than ever before is...are you ready for this? Garlic."

Jeff went on to explain. "Now I know, I know...you're thinking to yourself, 'What?? *Garlic?* That's a good way to *end* a relationship, not make it better.' I know you think I'm joking or making this up, but I'm dead serious. This really works."

Jeff continued, "Just try it. It will take your ability to speak the Language of the Heart to your spouse to the next level. I don't recommend trying this with your boss or coworkers. So, the next time you guys want to do something special for your spouse, go to the grocery store and buy some garlic cloves. Bring them home and when you walk in the door, tell her you want to try something new together. Now most people don't know this, but raw garlic (along with another ingredient I'll discuss in a moment) has a substance in it called PttH (polytetratimhydrozilene), which actually causes a reaction almost indistinguishable from physical attraction. If she will eat just two cloves with the other ingredient, she will experience an almost immediate sense of attraction to you and a bonded feeling toward your relationship. I know, I know, you don't believe me. But let me explain about the other ingredient and it will make more sense."

Sensing the congregation's anticipation, Jeff asked, "What is the other ingredient, you ask? Well, it has a dual purpose. One is chemical and the other is practical. As we all know, garlic is notorious for creating a horrible aftertaste and long-lasting bad breath. In fact, I know this was probably your number one objection when I mentioned garlic. But with this other ingredient, all of that changes and the garlic aftertaste and bad breath completely disappear. The other ingredient is...wait for it...*sugar*. By rolling the cloves in sugar for at least five minutes before you eat them, the chemical composition of the garlic will completely change and the bad taste will be eliminated. The sugar bonds with the garlic and releases the PttH to create that strong sense of attraction and that bonded feeling toward each other."

Well, I responded to Jeff by saying, "Wait a minute. How many of you are buying this? It sounds possible, doesn't it? How many of you think that this is total baloney? If you think this is total baloney, you're right, because it is! None of this is true. We made it all up. If you think you found the silver bullet for improving relationships, you'll be disappointed. Improving relationships takes a lot of work."

This was my way of introducing the concept of the Baloney Factor. There are people who are often simply "full of baloney." There are people who will tell you anything. There are people who will talk a good fight, as the saying goes, but when it is time to do something, you can't find them. There are people who promise all kinds of things and then never come through. I call this the Baloney Factor.

It shows in people who will tell you all sorts of things about how smart they are, or how successful they are. They'll brag about how much experience they've had and often the truth is they are full of baloney. There are people who tell you long stories about themselves and you'll walk away quite impressed, but deep down inside you know that something isn't exactly right, and you end up not trusting them. That damages the relationship.

Many years ago I knew a couple that were trying to have a baby and couldn't, so they decided to adopt a child. They ended up adopting a child from South Korea. This couple and I had a mutual friend who told me that he was going over to their home that night to babysit my friend's child. I asked him, "Why are you going over to babysit?" He replied, "Because I speak Korean."

What this guy (lets call him "Ron") didn't know about me was that I was in a high school gym class years earlier with a guy from South Korea. Every day in our gym class we started by waiting in groups. He was in my group, and one day, as we were waiting for our instructor, I asked him to teach me something in Korean. So he taught me "How are you?"

Fast forward to my conversation with Ron. I said, "So then you must know how to ask, 'How are you?' in Korean." (I actually used the Korean words.) Anyone who says they know a language has to know "how are you" because it is normally the first and most basic thing you learn in any language. When I asked Ron that question, he turned many shades of green and finally said he didn't know. At that moment he knew that I knew he was full of baloney.

That's what happens to people who are full of baloney. They almost always get caught, but they don't always know they are being found out. Most of the time no one calls such people on it. But in your mind, you just know these people are full of baloney. Once you are aware of this, certain things begin to happen. You don't trust this person any more and you don't believe what they say, or take what they say with a grain of salt. Or you recognize what they are telling you is partially or completely untrue. They have little to no credibility with you.

As a result, people who are full of baloney wonder why they don't get that job or that promotion. They wonder why they go through multiple friendships or their kids won't obey them. Because of the Baloney Factor, they often struggle and have challenges in their marriage. Marriage is based upon trust, and if that trust is compromised in the slightest, there will be problems.

The person who is full of baloney doesn't realize that other people know the truth. They believe they still have you believing the stories and the baloney. In fact, many times they actually believe the baloney themselves. They've been doing this for so long that they have fooled themselves. The problem is they are the only ones who are fooled; others are not.

Nothing improves when someone lacks trustworthiness. Such a person continues to represent untruths and is not trusted by many people. In fact, this person is unaware and oblivious to the whole situation until they get caught, and then the whole house of cards falls apart; especially if they've been living a secret life.

So why do people do this? It often begins as a way to have people think highly of you. If other people think that you're something, then maybe you will think you are something. For a while, it works, until people figure it out. They won't confront you until it becomes an important issue, and so you go along putting out the baloney and wondering why people don't want to help advance your life. The reason is that you can't be trusted.

Another reason people do this is because it is often a short cut. It's a short cut to really knuckling down and actually doing the work. It's easier to talk about how much you have accomplished than to actually accomplish it; or to talk about how much you know than to actually study, go to school, read the books and really know it. It is easier to know a little bit about something and talk as if you know it all, than to be humble and admit that you don't know what you don't know. Part of the factor behind this is, again, low self-esteem coming out as pride and confidence. For some, bragging is the only accomplishment of their lives and it gives them a false sense of value. The problem is the Baloney Factor doesn't work. What works is knowing our value is found in Christ and we don't need to appear to be something we aren't because we are loved and valued by Him.

Another example of the Baloney Factor is when someone is living a secret life. This can be done in a variety of ways but it always gets down to the same basic thing. Someone lives what appears on the outside an upstanding life. However, in private, when no one else is looking, they live an entirely different life, which is usually filled with sin. I have seen this so many times I've lost count; but the vast majority of the time, they get caught. One of the reasons for being caught is when someone lives a secret life, they must tell lies; sometimes for months or even years. To lie that much, they must have a very good memory. However, those who are hearing the lies only need to notice a couple of times when things don't add up. At that point their radar is listening for more lies, and they do find more. Liars are not very good at lying. They think lying is a short cut to happiness. If they were more disciplined, they would work at living a life of integrity, which brings greater happiness, but that discipline takes *work*. I have seen people carry on secret lives by having extramarital affairs, and in my experience, they always get caught, and every relationship they have becomes damaged.

Some lie about their secret life because they think they can handle it on their own, or there is no hope for them, which is absolutely not true. Anything that has you in its grip, whether it is an addiction or some other destructive activity, can have solutions. If you think your situation is hopeless, you are absolutely wrong and you need to seek help from a pastor or a professional Christian counselor because they will have real answers for your struggle.

It should be noted that there is redemption from secret lives. I have seen many marriages restored even though there had been affairs. But to do that requires counseling and total honesty going forward. In addition, there is forgiveness in Jesus. Because of the death and resurrection of Jesus Christ, you can be totally forgiven, washed and cleansed. Because of Jesus, you can start all over again.

The Baloney Factor can be many things. It can be people who brag and try to sell you a bunch of baloney about themselves or what they can do. It can be that they rarely keep their promises. It can be they just tell lies or live a secret life. All of this or any part of this is baloney, and it damages the relationships we have in our lives. Relationships, in order to be successful, demand honesty, because without honesty, relationships struggle every time. There is no shortcut to trustworthiness because it communicates you are dependable and reliable, and these are the hallmarks of healthy relationships.

HONESTY IS STILL THE BEST POLICY

"Truthful lips endure forever, but a lying tongue lasts only a moment." – Proverbs 12:19

This verse is telling us that truthfulness leaves a legacy. If you want to positively affect all the relationships in your life for the future, be an honest and truthful person. This verse is telling us the Baloney Factor doesn't work; it is short-lived. However, truthfulness will endure and build lasting relationships. You cannot get around this important Biblical principle. Look at what Jesus had to say about this in the Sermon on the Mount:

> *"Again, you have heard that it was said to those of ancient times, 'You shall not swear falsely, but carry out the vows you have made to the Lord.' But I say to you, do not swear at all, either by heaven, for it is the throne of God, or by the earth, for it is His footstool, or by Jerusalem, for it is the city of the great King. And do not swear by your head, for you cannot make one hair white or black. Let your word be 'Yes, Yes' or 'No, No'; anything more than this comes from the evil one."*
> *– Matthew 5:33-37*

Jesus recognizes here the Commandment indicates you and I should always be truthful. The Commandment applies to our lives. However, some of the religious leaders took what was said in this Commandment, about bearing false witness, and expanded it to oaths and vows as an expression of carrying it out. Jesus kicks things up a notch in this verse, which He often does. He says to not make an oath to tell the truth. Does that mean if you are in a courtroom and they ask you to put your hand on the Bible, you are not to swear to tell the truth? Not at all. Dr. Frederick Dale Bruner notes that Jesus is talking about our personal relationships and not addressing the issues of the State. Remember, Jesus once said, "Render to Caesar the things that are

Caesar's." In Lutheran theology, Martin Luther would remind us this is the separation of the Kingdoms. Jesus is talking about our personal relationships and not the State. What about marriage vows? He is saying keep your promises simple: "I do."

The point Jesus makes is that discipleship applies to speech. He says we should not say things like "I swear I am telling the truth" or "I swear on a stack of Bibles or on my mother's grave." He says do not swear by your head because you cannot make one hair white or black. Yes and No are enough.

Jesus says He wants us to guard against habitual swearing or as we've been saying, the Baloney Factor. Jesus says our conduct and words should always be truthful – so truthful that we never would have to swear we are being truthful.

"Do not lie to one another, seeing that you have stripped off the old self with its practices and have clothed yourself with the new self, which is being renewed in knowledge according to the image of its Creator." – Colossians 3:9-10

Here, the Apostle Paul is addressing the church and telling us one of the reasons we should not lie. In Christ we are a new creation. As we said in a previous chapter, we now have a new heart. Because of Jesus Christ, we are a new creation and we are to live differently. Paul says here that in Christ we are to live out the image of the Creator in whose image we have been created.

We must throw away the way we have done things in the past. In the Language of the Heart, we learn that truthfulness is essential in all aspects of our lives. When we are truthful in the big things and especially in the little things, we build trust with those around us, and this trust leads to respect. Then all of our relationships are improved. It has been said you know the character of someone by what they do when no one is watching. When this becomes our standard, it will elevate us to important levels of integrity and will improve every relationship.

When we function with high levels of integrity in our families, we find that so much trust is developed even our children learn to follow our leadership. They know whatever Mom or Dad asks of them must be for their total well-being, because they trust their parents so much. There are less arguments in a marriage between a man and a woman because with high integrity comes a trust in knowing the other spouse's motives are pure. When we are trustworthy at work, people will follow our lead; they know we are doing what is best for the company and all concerned. Trustworthiness is an essential value of the Language of the Heart.

So how do we get started? You can ask those around you this important question: "Am I full of baloney?" If they say yes, spend some time listening and learning how and what they have observed. Don't become defensive but practice active listening, and learn and understand what they are saying. Ask those who have identified this trait in you to point it out when they see you doing this in the future, and take their counsel with joy because you will be growing. Spend some time with God and ask Him to change your heart. Ask Him to give you a new heart that you can only have in Jesus Christ.

Additionally, make up your mind to always tell the truth and keep your promises. Ask God to help you do this. Ask others to point out the times when you don't. Often we have fooled ourselves and lied to ourselves so much that we can't see these things we are doing. Finally, remember there is hope. God is the God of second chances. You see, God became a man in Jesus Christ and died on a cross and was raised again from the dead so that you and I could be forgiven and renewed. Because of Jesus, we can stand before God as if we have never sinned.

It took a long time for Thomas Edison to develop the light bulb, and it took 24 hours to create just one bulb. When Edison and his group of scientists created that first bulb, he handed it to a young boy to take upstairs. The young boy, in fact, was very careful climbing the stairs with that bulb, but he dropped it at the top of the stairs and the bulb was destroyed. So, Edison and his team again began to work for 24 hours to create a second bulb. At this point you would think Edison would carry this second bulb upstairs himself, but that is not what he did. Instead Edison gave this new bulb to the same boy to be delivered upstairs.[8] This is a picture of forgiveness; what God has done for us in Christ Jesus. Through His cross, we have forgiveness and an opportunity for a second chance. If we have been someone who has been living out the Baloney Factor, we leave that behind and start a new life of honesty and integrity, which will help to improve every relationship in our lives. This is what God wants to do with you and me. He wants to give us a second chance, and this is possible because of Jesus Christ. You might have blown it in the past, but because of Jesus, you can start all over again. Because of Jesus, you can come home and start again.

CHAPTER EIGHT
AVOIDING SHAMING WORDS

Sometimes language can be very subtle, especially shaming language. Many times we do not notice that we are receiving it, and other times we don't recognize that our words to others are filled with shame. Perhaps as you were growing up, there was someone who used words that shamed you! And ever since, you have responded in the same way. A parent might have called you lazy or said you wouldn't amount to anything. A teacher could have told you that you were dumb and you would never go to college. Maybe you have been trying to prove them wrong, or you have believed what they said and ended up living it out. No matter how you responded, you have had a wound in your heart that has affected many of the life decisions you have made. This wound has also contributed to how you respond and deal with others at home and elsewhere.

WORDS OF SHAME DESTROY

Shame is different from guilt. Guilt says "I have done something wrong," but shame says "there is something wrong with me." We can receive and give these messages in many different ways. Sometimes it's through direct comments, and sometimes even through facial expressions and reactions. Often, it is done very subtly; to the point we don't even know that we're doing it or receiving it. But at other times it is overt.

Some parents shame their children with words comparing them to their siblings or to the parents' dreams and expectations:

- "You were a mistake."
- "You could never do what your sister/brother does."
- "You've ruined my life."
- "We are all disappointed in you."

Being shamed as a child has an impact on who you become as an adult. Dr. Jane Middelton-Moz, Ph.D.[9] says:

1. Adults shamed as children are afraid of vulnerability and fear exposure of self.
2. Adults shamed as children may suffer extreme shyness, embarrassment and feelings of being inferior to others. They don't believe they make mistakes. Instead, they believe they are mistakes.
3. Adults shamed as children fear intimacy and tend to avoid real commitment in relationships. These adults frequently express the feeling that one foot is out of the door, prepared to run.
4. Adults shamed as children may appear either grandiose and self-centered, or seem selfless.
5. Adults shamed as children feel that, "No matter what I do, it won't make a difference. I am and always will be

worthless and unlovable."

6. Adults shamed as children frequently feel defensive when even minor negative feedback is given. They suffer feelings of severe humiliation if forced to look at mistakes or imperfections.

7. Adults shamed as children frequently blame others before they can be blamed.

8. Adults shamed as children may suffer from debilitating guilt. These individuals apologize constantly. They assume responsibility for the behavior of those around them.

This kind of shame can cause someone to go into a type of hiding, even to the point of having and living out a secret life. But shaming doesn't have to have such dramatic results in our lives. The results can be milder.

Several years ago I noticed something strange had begun to happen to me in the way I made decisions. I noticed I was having difficulty making simple decisions. For example, I had a difficult time deciding between soup or salad on the menu in a restaurant. I asked a pastor friend why I was having this problem and what his thoughts were. My friend said he thought it was because I had been criticized a great deal. After some thought, I realized he was correct. In the previous years, I had some friends who were highly critical of each other and me. It was like a competition amongst these people. When anyone did something, one of them would have comments like "Why did you buy that shirt?" or "I didn't think you would understand that lecture." In other words, it was a very shaming experience.

A year later, the end result was finding myself paralyzed in making some of the simplest decisions. This kind of shaming was saying "there is something wrong with you" or "you aren't smart enough" or "you are not sophisticated" and so forth.

In a previous congregation where I served some years ago, I had a family in crisis. The wife had left and taken the children with her. She described her husband as oppressive and dictatorial and she'd had enough. I asked, and was granted, permission to speak with him. He shared his side of the situation with me. He was a successful businessman who travelled internationally much of the time. I could see that this man was a very strong and powerful personality, knowing little about the Language of the Heart. After we were done, he commented, "Oh, by the way, that city that you mentioned in your sermon? Well, it is not a small town but a huge city with millions of people." Do you see what he was doing? Here, in the middle of his marital and family crisis, he was shaming me. He was pointing out that he was smarter and knew more than I did. He was alone in his crisis and lashing out at me. It really is true that "hurt people hurt people."

This may appear to be subtle, but it is not. When you start thinking of all the times others have done this to you, you become amazed at how often you've been shamed. You don't always recognize it right away, and sometimes you never do, but have swallowed the shame and it's one more wound that is difficult to identify.

This shaming affects our lives and relationships. Often we react to shaming by giving it back to others. Shaming leads to arguments and fights. Shaming causes us to become defensive, making the argument more intense and louder. When we give this kind of shaming, the words of shame given overtly or subtly; damage and destroy the relationships in our lives. Shaming is toxic in our relationships and will always lead to damage.

We need to know the power of our language and how we speak.

"For all of us make many mistakes. Anyone who makes no mistakes in speaking is perfect, able to keep the whole body in check with a bridle. If we put bits into the mouths of horses to make them obey us, we guide their whole bodies. Or look at ships: though they are so large that it takes strong winds to drive them, yet they are guided by a very small rudder wherever the will of the pilot directs. So also the tongue is a small member, yet it boasts of great exploits. How great a forest is set ablaze by a small fire!" – James 3:2-5

Our tongue is like a rudder on a ship; a massive ship weighing thousands of tons controlled by the ever so small rudder. Our lives and relationships are controlled by what we say, and the health of our relationships will be determined by what we say and how we say it. Will we speak words of grace or words of shame? In the Language of the Heart, it is vital we understand his. This means to speak with people using unconditional love.

In the Book of James, the writer speaks of the power of the tongue in these words:

"With it we bless the Lord and Father, and with it we curse

those who are made in the likeness of God. From the same mouth come blessing and cursing. My brothers and sisters, this ought not to be so. Does a spring pour forth from the same opening both fresh and brackish water? Can a fig tree, my brothers and sisters, yield olives, or a grapevine figs? No more can salt water yield fresh." – James 3:9-12

We are told here to consider how we use our tongue. We are to use it to give praise to God but then we turn around and damage someone; someone who has value, someone who is made in the image of God. We are being asked to recognize what we are doing when we damage others with our shaming, and to recognize they have value, which should motivate us to stop shaming others.

In addition, we are encouraged here to be consistent in our speech and the only way we can be consistent is, once again, to have a new heart. Out of our old, broken, diseased heart, we will speak inconsistently, but with a new heart we can consistently speak words of grace. A spring does not put forth salt water and fresh water. With a new heart, we are meant to put forth fresh water, which are words of grace. We are to be consistent with our speech and we are not to have one type of speech at home and another in the world. It should be the same speech in all places, especially at home. Sometimes we have learned to give shame to others because we grew up in homes where shame was given in regular doses. We know no other way. Shame will destroy relationships.

WE ARE NOT DESIGNED FOR SHAME

The truth is we were never meant for shame. We were never meant to experience it, and we were never meant to express it to others. In the Garden of Eden, we were designed to know only grace, however, when sin came into the world shame also entered the world, and ever since it has been used to control, manipulate and oppress others.

"Therefore a man leaves his father and his mother and clings to his wife, and they become one flesh. And the man and his wife were both naked, and were not ashamed." – Genesis 2:24-25

Before sin came into the world, Adam and Eve could even be naked and there was no shame. We were not originally created with shame, but we now have an abundance of shame heaped upon us. The good news is that Jesus Christ has removed our shame. Through His death and resurrection, we are forgiven and freed from the shame of sin.

"Therefore, since we are surrounded by so great a cloud of witnesses, let us also lay aside every weight and the sin that clings so closely, and let us run with perseverance the race that is set before us, looking to Jesus the pioneer and perfecter of our faith, who for the sake of the joy that was set before Him endured the cross, disregarding its shame, and has taken His seat at the right hand of the throne of God. Consider Him who endured such hostility against Himself from sinners, so that you may not grow weary or lose heart." – Hebrews 12:1-3

The cross, in the days of Jesus, was a place of shame because it was the place for criminals to be punished. Talk about shame. The Son of God was made to appear as a criminal. He was laughed at as they put a crown of thorns on His head and mocked Him. They put a robe on Him as if He were a king, just to mock and shame Him. Jesus knows what it is like to experience shame. In facing the devil, He was shamed as the devil said to Him, "…If you are the Son of God, throw Yourself down from this mountain and Your angels will rescue You." Notice the language used by the devil toward Jesus: "If You are the Son of God." This is shaming language because He was and is the Son of God. Matthew 4:6 (RSV)

But Jesus "disregarded the shame" – in some translations it says He "despised" the shame. The term "despising" or "scorning" derives from a Greek word means that Jesus was ignoring the fact that the cross was shameful, because He was focused on the joy set before Him. And you are that joy. The joy for Jesus is that you and I could be set free and find new life in Him; we could be washed and have a new beginning is the joy set before Him.

JESUS CAME TO DESTROY THE SHAME WHICH DESTROYS US!

Because of what Jesus Christ has done on the cross, our sins are removed and we are forgiven. We can stand before God as if we have never sinned. That sounds like a removal of shame. Now we are no longer called "good for nothing" or "worthless" – now we are called Sons and Daughters of the King. In Christ Jesus, the shame is removed. Now we can give those words of grace to others. We don't have to remain in the pattern of having been shamed and giving shame to others. We can give words of grace because the greatest grace was given to us through Jesus Christ.

"There is therefore no condemnation for those who are in Christ Jesus." – Romans 8:1

A long time ago, a man by the name of Dr. J. Wilbur Chapman was in school preparing for the ministry. In those days D.L. Moody was a very famous pastor and evangelist. Chapman had been moved by the preaching and teaching of Moody, and began to follow him wherever he would go to hear him preach. At one of those churches where Moody was preaching, Chapman was able to ask Moody some questions. He told Moody he was uncertain if he would go to heaven. So Moody shared with him a passage of scripture from John 5:24 (RSV) which reads, "Truly, truly, I say to you, he who hears My word and believes Him who sent Me, has eternal life; he does not come into judgment, but has passed from death to life." Moody questioned Chapman and asked if he believed in the Son of God. Chapman said he did. Moody went on to ask Chapman if he would be condemned, and Chapman said he did not know and this was his struggle. D.L. Moody then said, "See here, young man, whom are you doubting?" Chapman started to realize he was doubting Christ Himself. Later he would say that this was a new realization for him and he never doubted after that moment.[10]

In Christ, we hear the good news that God has become a man

in Jesus and died on a cross, so you and I might have eternal life; not because of the good things we have done, but because of what Jesus has done for us at the cross. This is called the grace of God, which is unearned and unmerited favor, and we can give this grace away to others through the way we speak to them. This is the Language of the Heart.

CHAPTER NINE
BOUNDARIES

Many years ago, Jackson Browne wrote the lyrics to the song "Running on Empty."[11] Sometimes this describes our lives. There are so many pressures in life and many of us feel like we are *running on empty*. There was a time in our lives when we felt full and in control. We can remember a time when we felt adequate. However, if you have lived life for a time, you often find that life has a way of beating you down and you end up feeling like you are *running on empty*.

There are many reasons our tanks become empty. One such reason is we are often burning the candle at both ends. Sometimes this is because we have over-committed ourselves. While at other times, it is just the demands of life create a situation where we have more to do than we have time or the ability to do it. Sometimes, it is because we find it impossible to say "No."

LEARNING TO SAY "NO!"

Many people think the loving thing to do is to constantly

rescue other people from their irresponsibility. They take ownership of the continual mistakes other people make. They step in when someone is consistently making bad choices and rescue them from the consequences; believing, in fact, this is the loving thing to do.

Often this gets started when we are parenting children. Of course, when children are young they need adult supervision. They make poor choices and are capable of doing things that hurt themselves. So, we as parents have to take precautions. We put them in car seats and put gates in front of stairs. We put covers over electrical sockets and fences around swimming pools. The idea is that when they become older, we can remove these items because they will know better and they will make responsible decisions. So what do we do if they never mature? What if they never really grow up? What do we do if they continue to act like a child and need adult intervention?

What many parents do is keep treating their grown children as if they were still young children. We rescue them and function as the responsible party in many situations. We bail them out of the problem; not allowing them to own it themselves, because we don't want them to feel the pain of the consequences. Many parents believe helping them avoid consequences is the loving thing to do. However, it is not. When we do this long enough, we begin to *run on empty*. There is a name for this and it is called "enabling." This is done in all sorts of relationships from parents with adult children, to friendships, and even with our spouse. Some of us *run on empty* because we think loving others is to take ownership of their mess. An enabler is a person who knows when something negative is going on, tolerates it, and even takes over the responsibility to solve the problem for the other person. It creates an atmosphere where the other person can continue to do that which is irresponsible. Many have done this for several years and have set in place an environment where it will be difficult to bring change. Many do this out of a false understanding of love and compassion. Instead, all the enabler is doing is making the other person handicapped. This other person grows weaker and weaker in the months and years to come. Down deep in the heart of the enabler, they know something is wrong, but will not muster the wherewithal to change the pattern of enabling.

ARE YOU AN ENABLING PERSON?

Here are a few questions that might help you determine if you are an enabling person:

- Have you loaned money repeatedly and were never paid back?
- Have you paid for an education and/or job training which never resulted in a career?
- Have you finished a job or project that they failed to complete themselves because it was easier than trying to make them do it?
- Have you paid bills they were supposed to have paid themselves?
- Have you accepted part of the blame for their addictions or behavior?
- Have you avoided talking about negative issues – walking

on eggshells?

- Gone along with excessive use of alcohol? Made excuses for their drug use?
- Have you bailed them out of jail or paid for their legal fees?
- Have you given them multiple second chances and nothing changes?
- Have you wondered how they get money for the things they want but can't pay their own bills?
- Have you ever "called in sick" for them, lying about their symptoms to the boss?
- Have you threatened to throw them out and didn't?
- Have you noticed that things are missing from your home like money and other valuables?
- To put it simply, your helping is hurting.[12]

One time I had a father come to see me who was telling me all of the problems he was having with his post-high school son. Finally, he told me how his son was drinking a great deal, and then he mentioned how his son had recently smashed up his car badly. I asked the dad what he had done about this and he told me he had the car repaired. I asked, "Why did you do that?" The father replied, "Because he needed a car to get to work." Then I said, "It would have been cheaper for you to just go down to that bar he goes to and buy him a round of drinks." I was only trying to make a point because I went on to explain that he was enabling, and as long as he continued to do it, nothing would get any better.

So let's have a Definition and make a Distinction:

- **"Helping"** is doing something for someone else that they are not capable of doing for themselves.
- **"Enabling"** is doing things for someone else that they can and should be doing for themselves (Allison Bottke, *Setting Boundaries with your Adult Children*). Ibid

So for many of us one of the reasons we are *running on empty* is because we are constantly enabling others in our lives. Too often, we think that this is the loving thing to do but in reality we are really harming the other person. We are keeping them handicapped and incapable. They will never grow and develop as they should as long as we continue to enable them. We need to learn to be able to say "NO!"

"We must no longer be children, tossed to and fro and blown about by every wind of doctrine, by people's trickery, by their craftiness in deceitful scheming. But speaking the truth in love, we must grow up in every way into Him who is the head, into Christ." – Ephesians 4:14-15

What does this mean? This means sometimes we have to say "No" to that person we love, who is acting irresponsibly. It might mean allowing consequences to do the teaching. It has been said, "the people who love you the most are the ones who tell you what you don't want to hear." Saying "No" can be one of the most loving words you could ever utter.

ENMESHMENT

Many people in their enabling become what we would call "enmeshed." Enmeshment happens when personal boundaries are diluted and watered down. When this takes place in families with parents being enmeshed with children, it is sometimes a sign of the parents' needs in the relationship.

In enmeshment, we need to break the pattern. First, we need to recognize it is not normal or healthy; it is dysfunctional and damaging. We need to understand boundaries are essential and desperately needed. We need to understand boundaries are there to protect us and to guard us. Those boundaries are life-affirming. Dr. Henry Cloud and Dr. John Townsend[13] make a distinction between hurt and harm. A good parent will allow their child to be hurt if it means protecting them from a greater harm. So for example, if a parent pulls a daughter's hair to prevent her from running into the street and being struck by a car, it is not cruel. It might hurt, but it saved the girl from something of far greater pain and harm. A loving parent must sometimes allow their children to experience some hurt to protect them from greater harm. So, when we give a child a "time out" or take away some privilege in order to teach a child how to properly and safely behave, they might cry and feel that we are harming them, but in reality, we are guiding them and protecting them from greater harm in the future.

So wouldn't it be great if there was something in our relationship with others that could give us that kind of protection? Well there is, and it is called "BOUNDARIES." Jesu had boundaries. Practically every encounter He had with the religious leaders of His day was an example of setting boundaries and saying "No."

In order to achieve this, you might even need professional help. If someone in your life has serious addiction issues, get help. If someone in your life has a serious mental health problem, get help. There are many things in this realm you cannot handle alone and it all begins with you saying, "I am going to have boundaries," and then get the appropriate support. When you do this, your tank can be filled again. Having boundaries in life is being healthy and will help in developing functional relationships. This is what we teach in the Language of the Heart.

JESUS TOOK TIME TO REST AND BE RENEWED

One of the reasons some people *run on empty* is because many people are constantly fixing other people and taking responsibility for them. This enabling will empty your tank. However, the fast pace of life and hectic schedules we keep will also empty our tanks. We need to have and set boundaries, but we also need to find rest. In addition to making time for days off and taking vacations, what we really need is time for prayer. Taking time to rest in Christ through prayer can help to fill our tank. Look at this verse:

"In the morning, while it was still very dark, He got up and went out to a deserted place, and there He prayed. And Simon and his companions hunted for Him. When they found Him, they said to Him, "Everyone is searching for You." He answered, "Let us go on to the neighboring towns, so that I may proclaim the message there also; for that is what I came

to do." – Mark 1:35-38

Now it seems to me that if Jesus needed to pray, then we need it even more. The demands of ministry were all around Him. Crowds of hurting people followed Him everywhere He went, and the demands were great. What did He do? He got up early in the morning and prayed.

I am convinced that more time spent in prayer is essential for us to have our tank filled. I pray a great deal – but I know I could pray more. I think my being a Type A person is my biggest challenge in prayer. It can be difficult for me to pray because it means I am giving the problem over, and Type A's don't usually give problems over to anyone. However, what I have found is when I do give it over to the Lord in prayer, I know I am not alone. By casting the burden on the Lord, I am reminded He hasn't forgotten me. When I do this, I find these are the times when I get to watch Him work and do amazing things.

So, in this text, it says Jesus got up early in the morning and prayed. What would He have been praying for? Well, we know in the Garden of Gethsemane He was praying for strength to face the cross. So maybe in this example in Mark, Jesus was praying for strength for the day of ministry ahead. This causes us to focus on the nature of Jesus' prayers. One theologian wrote, "If I could hear Jesus praying for me in the next room, I would not fear a million enemies – Distance makes no difference. He is praying for you and me now."[14]

The Bible says:

"For there is one God and there is one mediator between God and men, the man Christ Jesus who gave Himself as a

ransom for all..." – 1 Timothy 2:5-6a (RSV)

In other words, Jesus is praying for you to the Father. Have you ever thought of that? As you go through your day, Jesus is praying for you. As you sleep at night, Jesus is praying for you. As you face the challenges of this life, Jesus is praying for you. Just knowing this and joining with Him in prayer, by spending time with Him as He prays for you, will fill your tank.

CHAPTER TEN
DON'T GO IT ALONE

One of the reasons some people struggle to learn the Language of the Heart is because they often try to go it alone in life. We live in a culture that honors and celebrates independence and self-reliance. Self-sufficiency is a highly prized virtue. Generally speaking, these are good traits to have in one's life. Certainly, every aspect of society and our lives are strengthened when these values are pursued. However, the problem begins when these are the only values lived out. They cause many people to be successful, but the downside of an over-reliance on these values most often leads to circumstances that are not so uplifting.

A RELATIONSHIP WITH GOD

When self-reliance and self-sufficiency are primary goals, they lead many to live lives of isolation. You and I were never created by our God to be totally self-reliant or self-sufficient. Instead, we were meant to be primarily God-reliant. We were meant to have a dependence on the God of heaven and earth with Him at the center of our lives. This is His desire for our lives. He longs to have a relationship with us. Just imagine what it would be like if, after you raised your children to adulthood, they never wanted to have anything to do with you. The only time they'd talk with you would be to ask you for your help or money. Wouldn't that break your heart? God is no different and we are created in His image. One of the basic principles of the Language of the Heart is that God must be at the center of our lives. It is essential to have a relationship with God, and only way we are able to have that relationship with God, is through Jesus Christ.

Who is better able to guide and lead our lives: Someone who knows all things and can see into the future? Someone who has all power and authority? Someone who loves you more than anyone has ever loved you? This, of course, is God, who sees and controls the future. God is better able to lead our lives than we are – we cannot even know what the next hour will bring.

In addition to having a relationship, He wants to give us eternal life, which is given by Him through Jesus Christ and His death and resurrection. Sometimes this is difficult to understand! When I was in high school, I was a Fuller Brush Man, going door-to-door selling household products from the Fuller Brush Company. One time I knocked on a door, which was answered by a man. I started my sales spiel, but he wasn't interested. Instead, he asked, "Young man, if you were to die tonight, would you go to heaven?" I said I wasn't sure.

He asked again, "Young man, if you were to die and stand before God tonight, what would you tell Him as to why He should let you into His heaven?" I replied, "I went to Sunday School all my life. I have been confirmed. I go to church every Sunday and I try to help people and I live a moral life."

The man explained this would never be enough. He explained that God is a holy God and cannot be in the presence of imperfection. God became a man in Jesus, died on a cross and was raised again from the dead. The Bible says that without the shedding of blood there is not forgiveness (Leviticus 17:11 and Hebrews 9:22, RSV). So God came, in Jesus Christ, and shed His blood. When we put our faith and trust in Jesus as our Savior, He will wash us and cleanse us, and we can stand before God as if we have never sinned. This is how God gives us eternal life. Because of what Jesus did, we have eternal life and we learn a new way to live. Now we do good things not because we hope to earn heaven (because we can't). Now we do good things out of gratitude to God for what Christ has done for us at the cross. (John 3:16 and Ephesians 2:8-10)

We call this Amazing Grace because it is amazing that God would do this for us, and grace because we do not deserve it. In the Language of the Heart we now take this grace and we give it to others. We give this forgiveness and love to people in our relationships. Giving grace to others means to give someone "the benefit of the doubt." It means to refrain from shaming others and instead, giving words of encouragement. The grace of God not only shapes us into new people, but it is meant to cause us to live differently. We reject the world's philosophy of self-reliance and self-sufficiency and become God-reliant in our lives.

When we live according to the philosophy of self-sufficiency, we can become workaholics because, after all, it's all up to us, right? This not only turns us into workaholics, but also Type A people. A Type A person is one who is a hard charging, take-no-prisoners kind of person. It is often their way or the highway. In fact, I have met many people who have gone past a Type A distinction to become what I call Type A++ personality.

In the Language of the Heart, we say that with Christ being our Savior, we don't go it alone and now we have a new set of values. Instead of valuing money and using people, we use money and value people. Instead of pursuing power, fame or material reward, we focus on humility and service. In addition to having met so many Type A's who are very successful at work but failures at home, I also have met many people who are highly intelligent, well-educated and extremely successful; but their adult children will not have relationships with them. They themselves do not have deep or lasting relationships. The philosophy of self-reliance is just a shiny object and has nothing for us. However, we don't have to wait until it all falls apart for us to set a new course. In Christ, we have new values.

ALLOW OTHERS TO TEACH YOU

"A fool despises a parent's instruction, but the one who heeds admonition is prudent." – Proverbs 15:5

"There is severe discipline for one who forsakes the way, but one who hates a rebuke will die." – Proverbs 15:10

"Without counsel, plans go wrong, but with many advisers, they succeed." – Proverbs 15:22

What are these verses all saying? They are saying we must be open to instruction. Too often, we are stubborn and think we know better than others. Sometimes we think we are bulletproof or the smartest person in the room. When we think this way, we believe we can get close to the edge and nothing will happen to us. Bad things only happen to others who are not as smart or sophisticated as we are. This attitude shows we often lack a teachable spirit. We do this because of our pride.

"The LORD tears down the house of the proud, but maintains the widow's boundaries." – Proverbs 15:25

"Those who ignore instruction despise themselves, but those who heed admonition gain understanding. The fear (or respect) of the LORD is instruction in wisdom, and humility goes before honor." – Proverbs 15:32-33

These verses are foundational. Pride and arrogance keeps us from going to Jesus in the first place. Pride will always keep us from having a teachable spirit. When we think we are the smartest person in the room, we also think rules don't apply to us. We go on to believe we are not like other people and we can handle the problem without any help. This always leads to problems. In working with people when they have serious issues and problems in their lives, I find it most often begins with pride and arrogance.

We need to confess this to a trusted person. Find someone who could be a Christian mentor for you, someone who is strong in Christ and can listen. Share with them your struggle with pride and hubris. Allow them to speak into your life things that perhaps others have wanted to say in the past but never could. Ask them if you have a teachable spirit and be open to the answer.

Then, be open to learning and growing. Be in a Bible-based small group. Be in church every week. Go to a Christian counselor. Go to Cursillo; a three-day spiritual retreat which touches people at a deeper level. Go to a pastor. Go to a 12-step program for addiction. Allow these resources to teach you so you can grow. When we reject what any of these sources are trying to say to us, we find our lives become hard and difficult. This is because our pride and arrogance are getting in the way of what God really wants to do in our lives.

So many times I have had people come to me with problems. We have heard this saying many times: "Denial is not just a river in Egypt" – and it is true. Denial is one of the greatest forces in keeping our lives from getting better. Every addict I've known started off in denial, and the ones who got well were the ones who came to a place where they could be taught. Many marriages are in trouble because one spouse says he or she is not the one with the problem and counseling isn't needed. Nothing ever gets better as long as we remain in denial and cannot be taught.

THE NEED FOR CHRISTIAN COMMUNITY

We live in a society where we celebrate liberty and

individualism; living by "radical individualism." We actually believe we don't need too much support or other people in our lives. This causes us to live in isolation which leads to many problems in our lives. We were never designed by God to live in isolation. The truth is that deep within our souls, we long for community. However, because we believe in the culture of individuality, we are stuck and don't feel we can ever reach out. We are not meant to live in isolation. In the Language of the Heart, we learn we should never hide in isolation. The lesson here is, don't go it alone.

It is fascinating to learn that even science is discovering the value of community. For example, Dr. Sheldon Cohen of the Carnegie-Mellon University[15] discovered when people have a large number of social contacts, they actually have fewer colds. From the research I have seen, we find that those who are isolated have a higher suicide rate, or a five-fold greater risk of dying from disease and other causes. There are reams of information to show that being in a community will improve your health, level of joy, and sense of fulfillment.

In the life of the church, we are meant to support each other. We are meant to guide each other to places of spiritual health. We are meant to pray for each other. We are meant to care about each other. We are meant to look to our brothers and sisters in Christ as those who will give us support in times of need.

"My friends, if anyone is detected in a transgression, you who have received the Spirit should restore such a one in a spirit of gentleness. Take care that you yourselves are not tempted. Bear one another's burdens, and in this way you will

fulfill the law of Christ. For if these who are nothing think they are something, they deceive themselves." – Galatians 6:1-3

We need to be encouraged and to support each other. It is truly life affirming. Here is another word of encouragement for being in community:

"And let us consider how to provoke one another to love and good deeds, not neglecting to meet together, as is the habit of some, but encouraging one another, and all the more as you see the Day approaching." – Hebrews 10:24-25

Many years ago, there were miners trapped in a mine in Pennsylvania. They were trapped for three days in the Quecreek Mine in Somerset County. The mineshaft was full of water and they were 240 feet underground. The water was 55°F and they were at risk of dying because of hypothermia. Together, they made a decision of what they would do to survive until they were rescued. When someone was cold, they would gather together and huddle until they were warm. When one of them became discouraged, the others would encourage him. What a terrible ordeal – but they survived because of community. (Joel Smith and Bill White)[16]

THE CHURCH IS ESSENTIAL FOR YOUR LIFE

We need a place where we can be encouraged. This place is the church of the Lord Jesus Christ. Perhaps you are asking, "Why the church? Why do I need community in the church?" It is because only within God's family you are accepted with unconditional love. At home, you may feel merely tolerated.

Maybe with your friends, it's always "keeping up with the Joneses." In the church, you will be loved by God, and others will love you just as you are. We are not perfect at this, but we are constantly striving and working on it.

If you've ever spent an extended time with a family member or friend who is in the hospital, you see a picture of the church. In the waiting room, people support each other. They ask how their loved one is doing. There are no distinctions concerning wealth, race or accomplishment. Nor is there pride or arrogance in the room. People keep each other in prayer. When the doctor brings good news, they all rejoice, and when that same doctor brings bad news, they feel the pain together. This is part of what the church is meant to be, the place where we receive that kind of support and encouragement all the time. The truth is we really need it.

I would like to urge you to become a regular in worshipper in a Christian church. Many people say, "I don't need to go to church to have a relationship with God." Even if this is true (which it is not), many who say this don't ever end up having a relationship with God. Many who say this end up being the god of their own lives and this is why they do not go to church. But the truth is that we are commanded by God to worship Him weekly in Christian community. It is powerful to realize that Jesus worshipped on the Sabbath every week, as the Bible says, '... as was His practice." I think if Jesus corporately worshipped regularly, then certainly I should, too. The third commandment of God to Moses told the people that worship was something God commanded. It is not a suggestion or a recommendation, but a command from God. We need this in our lives because we leak. That is, we leak spiritually and need to be constantly replenished through God's Word. In fact, that is how faith is developed in us. In Romans 10:17 (RSV), it says:

"So faith comes from what is heard, and what is heard comes by the preaching of Christ."

We need to have the Word of God poured into our hearts and minds in order for us to grow and develop. It is certainly one of the ways we grow in the Language of the Heart.

The key is ***don't go it alone***. Our tanks get empty when we try to go it alone. When our pride and arrogance drive us and control us, we move into isolation and this is when we enter into the position of making significant mistakes. Our lack of a teachable spirit causes us to remain in this position of isolation and we make even more mistakes. Our tanks become empty and we become depleted.

We were never meant to live in isolation. We were designed for Christian community, where we learn to:

- Remove our pride
- Have a teachable spirit
- Grow
- Be honest about our brokenness
- Get the support and help we need

And, finally, invest in Christian community, where we have our lives filled with God's amazing grace and unconditional love through Jesus Christ – don't go it alone.

CONCLUSION

My great prayer is that this book has been helpful to you. My prayer is that it will assist you in improving every relationship in your life. It is important to recognize this cannot be the end of the process for you. Find ways to keep learning the Language of the Heart through reading other books dealing with relationships, attending classes, and studying the Word of God, the Bible. I have found that "lifelong learning" is vital to our lives so I encourage you to keep learning.

Perhaps this book has caused you to realize you need to make some positive changes. Perhaps it is time to start seeing a Christian therapist or a pastor. Entering this kind of process is an important step, because by taking this step you are beginning to deal with many of the issues that so often get in the way of healthy relationships. By seeing a Christian counselor or a pastor, you are beginning to deal with such things as pride and even denial. As you continue this process, you will learn how to deal with other issues that get in the way of having a healthy relationship. This will mean you will need to resist the temptation to be defensive, and you will need to have a teachable spirit so you can grow and improve your relationships.

This might even be the point at which you enter a 12-step or Celebrate Recovery program and work on the issues of addiction. Once again, by doing so, you will automatically start working on pride and denial and will be developing a teachable spirit. This step of dealing with addiction will be a "game changer" in all of your relationships. Some people only go half way. By this, I mean they will stop using let's say alcohol, but never go to a 12-step program, and therefore, they only solve part of the problem. While they might be sober; which is good, they have not done anything to deal with the other issues damaging their relationships. I call it a "dry drunk." Don't just put your toe in the water, jump in and grow in all areas of sobriety! Go to a 12-step or Celebrate Recovery program.

I encourage you to also start attending a Christian church which meets your needs and this, too, will help you grow and develop spiritually so you can be a healthier person. Several years ago, I borrowed from my friend, Dr. Hal Seed, something he calls "The Big Promise." The Big Promise says if you will put Jesus Christ as Lord and Savior of your life, go to church regularly (3-4 times a month), become involved in a small group, and find a place to serve the Lord in your church; your life will be better one year from now. I believe this is true because I have seen it happen. Find a church and make it your home.

In other words, we have been saying "don't go it alone" and get the help you need. Take these kinds of steps and you will find things can improve. Relationships can improve when we take the right actions and make the right changes. The biggest change is to have our hearts changed. This is where it really begins, and the only One who can change our heart is God. Through Jesus Christ, ask God to give you a new heart and then take the kind of steps we have outlined in this conclusion.

Too many people give up too soon. Too many run to divorce court too soon. I encourage you to take the steps we pointed to in this conclusion before you walk away. There is always hope. Don't give up too soon. Take this kind of action and you will be surprised at what can happen. And if the only thing happens is that you are changed and you grow, then it will be worth it. Give it a try.

ACKNOWLEDGMENTS

I am grateful to many people who have made this project become a reality. Thank you to Karin MacKrell, Sue Jorgenson, Taryn Coss, Jane Frost and Christina Vogt, who helped with editing and formatting over various periods of the project.

Thank you to Dr. Ed Ewart and Dr. Piper Glasier for their advice and counsel.

Thank you to my graphic artist and daughter, Astrid Steward Murphy, for the cover design of this book, Language of the Heart: Improving Every Relationship.

NOTES

Verses marked RSV are taken from the Revised Standard Version of the Bible from www.Biblegateway.com Harper Collins, Publishing, Zondervan Corp., New York, 1975-2017. All rights reserved.

NRSV bible verses unless otherwise indicated, all Scripture quotations are taken from the HOLY BIBLE, New Revised Standard Version NRSV Copyright © 1997 by World Publishing, Nashville, TN, www.worldpublishing.com All rights reserved.

For privacy reasons, some of the names in Language of the Heart have been changed.

ENDNOTES

[1] Joel Pankow, Pastor, The Thorn Bush and Apple Tree. Pastor Joel Pankow of Trinity Evangelical Church in Bayside, Michigan.

[2] Anthony T. Evans, Dr., Guiding Your Family in a Misguided World, The Story of Two Monks.

[3] Frederick Dale Bruner, Dr., Matthew: The Christbook, Matthew 1-12 Volume 1 of Matthew: A Commentary. Eerdmans Publishing, 2004.

[4] Ruth Schenk, The Kim Phuc Story. Permission to use by Southeast Outlook. Source: Ruth Schenk, "Napalm Attack Begins 36-year Journey to Faith and Forgiveness, "Southeast Outlook. www.PreachingToday.com. September 11, 2008.

[5] Kelly Clarkson, "Since You've Been Gone." Breakaway. RCA Records. 2004.

[6] Oliver Sacks, An Anthropologist on Mars. Penguin Random House Publishers, Vintage: 1 ed., 1996.

[7] Marty Williams, Pastor, Dr. of Family Ministries. Compilation of questions. infor@martinwilliamsorg

[8] James Newton, Uncommon Friends: Life with Thomas

Edison, Henry Ford, Harvey Firestone, Alexis Carrel and Charles Lindbergh. New York: Houghton Mifflin, 1989.

[9] Jane Middelton-Moz, Ph.D., Shame & Guilt: Masters of Disguise. Mount Pocono: Health Communications Inc., 1990.

[10] H.Y. Pickering, Copied for WholesomeWords.org from Twice-Born Men: True Conversion Records of 100 Well-known Men in All Ranks of Life compiled by HY. Pickering. London: Pickering & Inglis, (1930). Copyright @2017 Wholesome Words. All Rights Reserved.

[11] Jackson Browne, "Running on Empty." 1977.

[12] Allison Bottke, Setting Boundaries with your Adult Children. Eugene: Harvest House Publishers, 2008 (Used with permission Seedtime, 2015).

[13] Henry Cloud, Dr. and Dr. John Townsend, Boundaries, When to Say Yes, How to say No to Take Control of your Life. Grand Rapids: Zondervan Publishers, 1992.

[14] Lloyd John Ogilvie, Drumbeat of Love. Word Books Publisher, 1979.

[15] Sheldon Cohen, Prof., Perceived Stress Scale. Mindgarden, 1994. The PSS Scale is reprinted with permission of the American Sociological Association, from Cohen, S., Kamarck, T., and Mermelstein, R. (1983). (Eds.) The Social Psychology of Health, Newbury Park, CA: Sage, 1988.

[16] Joel Smith, Quoted in "Living the Call", www.sermoncentral.com Source: Bill White, Paramount, California; Citation: adapted from "Teamwork Helped Miners Survive Underground," CNN.com from PreachingToday.com. (7-28-02).

LANGUAGE OF THE HEART
IMPROVING EVERY RELATIONSHIP

ISBN 978-0-9600833-0-5